"A serious comedy about the mid[...]
man who doesn't know how to [...]
else, for that matter. At once rep[...] *Linda Vista* draws you into the shared plights of its dissatisfied characters with absolute assurance."

—TERRY TEACHOUT, *WALL STREET JOURNAL*

"Mr. Letts has created a profoundly personal, beautifully honest piece of work that deeply engages the audience . . . There's karaoke, lots of uninhibited sex, rich conversation, many laughs, and love. Much more love than appears at first glance."

—SAMUEL GARZA BERNSTEIN, *STAGE AND CINEMA*

"*Linda Vista* is a well-crafted dramedy with laughs and pathos in the right places . . . Letts's sharp dialogue and shipshape dramaturgy make for a smooth ride."

—DAVID COTE, *OBSERVER*

"Letts excels at character, dialogue, and psychology . . . In *Linda Vista*, the dramatic writing has a kinetic kick, the dialogue is potently funny, and the psychological dynamics are riveting in their accuracy."

—CHARLES MCNULTY, *LOS ANGELES TIMES*

"A very funny new play about a very sad man . . . Irresistible."

—GREG EVANS, *DEADLINE*

"Exceedingly funny . . . Letts has a tremendous gift for capturing misbehavior among and between the sexes . . . A keenly astute character study about a man in desperate need of a lifeline, cluelessly lost in the gravitational pull of middle age . . . We are with him, laughing and crying all the way."

—ROMA TORRE, NY1

LINDA VISTA

LINDA VISTA

Tracy Letts

THEATRE COMMUNICATIONS GROUP / NEW YORK / 2020

The publication of *Linda Vista* by Tracy Letts, through TCG's Book Program, is made possible in part by the New York State Council on the Arts with the support of Governor Andrew Cuomo and the New York State Legislature.

TCG books are exclusively distributed to the book trade by Consortium Book Sales and Distribution.

Library of Congress Control Numbers:
2019057729 (print) / 2019057730 (ebook)
ISBN 978-1-55936-971-8 (paperback) / ISBN 978-1-55936-924-4 (ebook)
A catalog record for this book is available from the Library of Congress.

Book design and composition by Lisa Govan
Cover design by John Gall
Cover photo: Shutterstock/sumikophoto

First Edition, August 2020

For Haskell

ACKNOWLEDGMENTS

Many thanks to all of the fine people—hundreds of them, actually—who helped realize the productions of *Linda Vista* at Steppenwolf in Chicago, Center Theatre Group in Los Angeles, and Second Stage in New York.

As is always the case with my plays, my director and dramaturg were instrumental in the creation of the work. So I give thanks to Dexter Bullard and Ed Sobel.

I was blessed with a phenomenal company of actors in all three cities. I'm deeply grateful to the contributions and deep commitment of Ian Barford, Tim Hopper, Kahyun Kim, Sally Murphy, Caroline Neff, Chantal Thuy, Jim True-Frost, Cora Vander Broek, and Troy West.

My designers always have a lot of helpful things to say. Thanks to Laura Bauer, Marcus Doshi, Todd Rosenthal, and Richard Woodbury. Chris Freeburg, David Franklin, Jim Harker, and all of their assistants, ran remarkably smooth operations.

We used Steely Dan music for our transitions. Tracking down and acquiring the rights to those recordings was a job of work. Very special thanks to Lindsay Allbaugh, Eric Sims, Nausica Stergiou, David Leinheardt, Sara Danielsen, Christie Evangelista, Reed Wilkerson, Billy Petersen, Alan Rosenberg, Irving Azoff, and the Estate of Walter Becker. And thanks to the man himself, Donald Fagen, for making it happen.

For good listening and wise counsel, I thank Anna D. Shapiro, Michael Ritchie, Jon Berry, Aaron Carter, Hallie Gordon, Dianne Nora, Laura Dupper, Juli Del Prete, and Ron Gwiazda. Valuable workshop help was provided by Dianne Doan, Sandra Marquez, and Rachel Sondag. Dear friends Bob Fisher, Loren Lazerine, Scott Morfee, David Pasquesi, and Jeff Still all made contributions, whether they know it or not. And Carrie Coon is the best first reader any writer could hope for.

Fifty: it is a dangerous age—for all men, and especially for one like me who has a tendency to board sinking ships. Middle age has all the scares a man feels halfway across a busy street, caught in traffic and losing his way, or another one blundering in a black upstairs room, full of furniture, afraid to turn on the lights because he'll see the cockroaches he smells. The man of fifty has the most to say, but no one will listen. His fears sound incredible because they are so new—he might be making them up. His body alarms him; it starts playing tricks on him, his teeth warn him, his stomach scolds, he's balding at last; a pimple might be cancer, indigestion a heart attack. He's feeling an unapparent fatigue; he wants to be young but he knows he ought to be old. He's neither one and terrified. His friends all resemble him, so there can be no hope of rescue. To be this age and very far from where you started out, unconsoled by any possibility of a miracle—that is bad; to look forward and start counting the empty years left is enough to tempt you into some aptly named crime, or else to pray. Success is nasty and spoils you, the successful say, and only failures listen, who know nastiness without the winch of money. Then it is clear: the ship is swamped to her gunwales, and the man of fifty swims to shore, to be marooned on a little island, from which there is no rescue, but only different kinds of defeat.

—PAUL THEROUX, *SAINT JACK*

Well the danger on the rocks is surely past
Still I remain tied to the mast
Could it be that I have found my home at last
Home at last
—WALTER BECKER AND DONALD FAGEN, "HOME AT LAST"

LINDA VISTA

Linda Vista had its world premiere at Steppenwolf Theatre Company (Anna D. Shapiro, Artistic Director; David Schmitz, Executive Director) in Chicago, on April 9, 2017. It was directed by Dexter Bullard. The scenic design was by Todd Rosenthal, the costume design was by Laura Bauer, the lighting design was by Marcus Doshi, the sound design was by Richard Woodbury; the dramaturg was Edward Sobel and the stage manager was Christine D. Freeburg. The cast was:

WHEELER	Ian Barford
PAUL	Tim Hopper
MICHAEL	Troy West
ANITA	Caroline Neff
MINNIE	Kahyun Kim
MARGARET	Sally Murphy
JULES	Cora Vander Broek

This production of *Linda Vista* opened at Center Theatre Group (Michael Ritchie, Artistic Director; Douglas C. Baker, Producing Director) in Los Angeles, on January 9, 2019. The creative team remained the same, with the following exception: the production stage manager was David S.

Franklin. The cast remained the same, with the following exception:

MINNIE   Chantal Thuy

This production of *Linda Vista* opened on Broadway at the Helen Hayes Theater on October 10, 2019. It was produced by Second Stage (Carole Rothman, President and Artistic Director; Casey Reitz, Executive Director) in association with Center Theatre Group. The creative team remained the same as the Center Theatre Group production, with the following exception: the production stage manager was James Harker. The cast remained the same, with the following exception:

PAUL   Jim True-Frost

CHARACTERS

WHEELER, fifty
PAUL, fifty
MICHAEL, mid-fifties
ANITA, mid-thirties
MINNIE, twenties
MARGARET, fifty
JULES, late thirties

SETTING

Various locations in San Diego.

Act One

SCENE 1

Wheeler's new apartment.
   Wheeler and Paul.

WHEELER: Thanks.

PAUL: You don't have that much stuff.

WHEELER: Know what I say when someone asks me to move their shit?

PAUL: What?

WHEELER: "No."

PAUL: Has anyone ever asked you? I wouldn't ask you.

WHEELER: Well, no, probably no one's ever asked me. But I can tell you what I *wouldn't* say, I *wouldn't* say, "Oh, hey, I'd love to help you out but I slammed my dick in a car door and I gotta go to the doctor."

PAUL: You wouldn't say that, huh?

WHEELER: Point is, I don't *lie*.

PAUL: You don't lie in response to a question no one's asked you?

WHEELER: Want to get a bite to eat? Want to get some Mexican? On me.

PAUL: I can't, Margaret and I have a dinner thing. Old friends of Margaret's. They're in town.

WHEELER: They're not staying with you, are they?

PAUL: Just tonight. They're in for a wedding tomorrow. So we're going out to dinner. Fleming's.

WHEELER: You seem enthusiastic.

PAUL: It's all right. It's fine. They're old friends and we don't have a lot in common anymore, you know?

WHEELER: That's why new friends are better than old friends.

PAUL: You think?

WHEELER: Cause of what you said, we lose whatever we had in common with old friends, we *change*. Why do we have to stick with old friends forever? They're not family. We should be able to just trade in old friends for new ones.

PAUL: What about loyalty?

WHEELER: Loyalty to an idea is better than loyalty to people.

PAUL: No. You believe that?

WHEELER: Loyalty to people is how you wind up camping with Hitler.

PAUL: And he was not a good camper. One thing with these friends, they're so conservative politically?

WHEELER: Which is exactly what I'm saying. Don't tell me they're Trump voters.

PAUL: I don't know, I'm afraid to bring it up.

WHEELER: You cannot be friends with these people. The problem with these racist cocksuckers isn't that they're doing too much OxyContin, it's that they need to do a whole lot more. I stopped trying to be polite about it.

PAUL: Were you trying to be polite about it?

WHEELER: And we're supposed to find middle ground with

these people. *What* middle ground, where is this ground in the middle? These people are so fucking stupid, they think human beings walked around with dinosaurs. I have to find middle ground with that? "No, sir, you're an idiot, I'd prefer not to meet you anywhere near the middle. I'll stay right here and you stay way over there on the stupid side." Aren't you obligated to deal with these assholes at work?

PAUL: Kind of an unwritten rule at City Hall, we never talk politics.

WHEELER: I was out to dinner with this girl and we were talking, turns out she comes from this big military family, like everybody in the family has served, and I hear this and I'm thinking, "Please don't say some dumb shit about the stupid border wall or NFL players taking a knee cause I just won't handle it well," and so I play it cool, y'know, "Thanks for their service," or whatever, and then I said, very concerned, "Too bad we're always stuck in these pointless bullshit wars, like too bad all these motherfuckers are dead for no good reason." And she went off on me! I said, "Didn't I say, 'Thanks for their service?' I'm on *their* side, I don't want these guys going off and dying, I think they should just stay anchored out there in the bay doing their dumb fucking maneuvers and doing, y'know, *pushups*."

PAUL: How'd that go over?

WHEELER: I got the check while she started singing "Proud to Be an American." And this girl, my God . . . like Ali MacGraw. I would've worn a MAGA hat if she'd let me do all my dirty things.

PAUL: Wow. Like *Goodbye, Columbus* Ali MacGraw?

WHEELER: More like *Convoy* Ali MacGraw.

PAUL: Ew, with the perm?

WHEELER: She didn't have a perm.

PAUL: Ali MacGraw had a perm in *Convoy*.

WHEELER: This girl did not have a perm.

PAUL: Then how is she like *Convoy* Ali MacGraw?

WHEELER: The essence. The essence of *Convoy* Ali MacGraw.

PAUL: When you say *Convoy* Ali MacGraw, I pretty much just picture that perm.

WHEELER: Well, stop picturing that.

PAUL: I don't get that, why'd they make her perm her hair? That long straight brunette hair was her signature, y'know?

WHEELER: The crooked front tooth was her signature. The long straight brunette hair was a *feature*, but the crooked front tooth was her signature.

PAUL: She was a sex addict, you know.

WHEELER: Really? How do you know?

PAUL: I don't have any inside information. She wrote it in her autobiography.

WHEELER: You read Ali MacGraw's autobiography?

PAUL: No.

WHEELER: She was a sex addict? That pisses me off.

PAUL: Why's that?

WHEELER: I never meet any female sex addicts. I've never once met a female sex addict. Where was I when Ali MacGraw was addicted to sex?

PAUL: You were about nine years old.

WHEELER: Don't play with numbers. There's a principle here.

PAUL: There's no guarantee she would've been into you at any age.

WHEELER: Isn't that the whole thing about a sex addict? They're not known for their discernment.

PAUL: The most hardcore sex addict still might not be into you.

WHEELER: What kind of addiction is *that*? C'mon. "Sex addict." Is that even a real thing? We start throwing around the word addiction for everything we do or use immoderately but does that really make it an addiction?

PAUL: I guess it depends on how you define—

WHEELER: Let me ask you. I don't even have to ask, I know the answer. When you were a kid, didn't you jerk off all the time?

PAUL: Sure.

WHEELER: Is that an addiction? When you were thirteen years old, were you *addicted* to jerking off?

PAUL: I'm *still* addicted to jerking off.

WHEELER: Up top.

(They slap a casual high five.)

Maybe Ali MacGraw just liked to fuck a lot. Should we criminalize her for that?

PAUL: I'm not criminalizing her. I didn't call her a sex addict.

WHEELER: You *just* called her a sex addict.

PAUL: She called *herself* a sex addict.

WHEELER: Well she's being too hard on herself. She shoulda just said, "Hi, I'm Ali MacGraw and I like to fuck a lot."

PAUL: Used to.

WHEELER: "Hi, I'm Ali MacGraw and I used to like to fuck a lot."

PAUL: What is this she's doing, is she on a commercial?

WHEELER: Yes, she is. "Hi, I'm Ali MacGraw and I used to like to fuck a lot, so when I use paper towels, I use Brawny."

PAUL: What does fucking a lot have to do with paper towels?

WHEELER: She's a celebrity spokesperson, the talent doesn't have to match the product. Remember Joe DiMaggio and Mr. Coffee? "Hi, I'm Joe DiMaggio, I hit .325 lifetime and have nine rings, so when I drink coffee, I make it in this cheap plastic piece of shit."

PAUL: Nine rings? Is that right?

WHEELER: Oh yeah. Fucking Yankees.

PAUL: You had a date. I didn't know you were dating.

WHEELER: I've had a couple dates.

PAUL: Anything look promising?

WHEELER: No, nothing serious, I'm really not looking. I mean there's the new girl at work. Anita.

PAUL: Anita, that's the brunette.

WHEELER: Yeah, you met her. The new girl. Not really brunette.

PAUL: You're going out with Anita?

WHEELER: No, we went to lunch. Just over to the food court.

PAUL: She seems great. I mean I barely met her.

WHEELER: She is great.

PAUL: She has ample breasts.

WHEELER: Very large breasts.

PAUL: I mean substantial.

WHEELER: Are we just looking for different ways to say big?

PAUL: Have you seen them?

WHEELER: We had a twenty-minute lunch at the food court, Paul. She didn't expose her bosom at the Lotus Express.

PAUL: I'm glad you're going out. I've been worried about you.

WHEELER: Why?

PAUL: You've been through a tough time.

WHEELER: Yeah, but I got this place now and I'm getting it together.

PAUL: How'd you find this place?

WHEELER: The internet.

PAUL: It's all right.

WHEELER: Anything's an improvement over the cot in my wife's garage. My kid looking out there in the morning like, "Who's the loser sleeping in the garage? Oh that's right, it's my *dad*."

PAUL: How many square feet?

WHEELER: I don't know, eight hundred, nine hundred. Eight hundred. Two bedrooms. And you got the pool out there.

PAUL: Right.

WHEELER: And you can see the ocean.

PAUL: You can?

WHEELER: Look through there.

PAUL: I am.

WHEELER: Stand here. Now stand up straight.

PAUL: What, is that it?

WHEELER: You're looking to the right of the silver building?

PAUL: Oh, there it is, got it.

WHEELER: Yeah, so there's a view.

PAUL: And did this furniture come with the place?

WHEELER: Yeah, you could get it with or without. I mean, what am I gonna do, go out and buy a bunch of furniture?

PAUL: You could.

WHEELER: Fuck that. This stuff is fine. *(Pause)* You want a beer?

(Paul hesitates.)

Have a beer. It's the least I can do.

PAUL: Sure, I got a few minutes.

WHEELER: You want a glass?

PAUL: No, that's okay.

WHEELER: The grocery store isn't far from here.

PAUL: That's good.

WHEELER: And that huge Vietnamese market. It's like the Walmart of Vietnamese markets.

PAUL: Here's to the new place.

WHEELER: The new place.

(They clink bottles.)

PAUL: This should make dating easier, right? A place to bring all your ladies. It's not like you could take them back to Kelly's garage.

WHEELER: I really should not be with a woman right now.

PAUL: Yeah, okay.

WHEELER: I mean it. It's hard for me right now to even just sit with a woman and have a conversation. I'm too old to pretend to be something I'm not and a lot of the things I *am* are not attractive. And this divorce has a way to go, and it's not nasty exactly, but I can see nasty from here.

PAUL: Really.

WHEELER: The money's turned into a sticking point. Which is strange.

PAUL: Yeah, cause you don't have any money.

WHEELER: I get that my kid's involved so I'm prepared to pay for that. But I sat down with Kelly and I threw out a number and she said, "You're not even close." I said, "What's your number?" And she wrote it down—I think she knew how outrageous it would sound spoken out into the world—and it was a number so high only dogs could hear it. So now we got arbitration and these asshole lawyers and it's a big fucking clusterfuck.

PAUL: This has been going on for more than a year.

WHEELER: *Two* years, this past Valentine's Day. The affair, the discovery of the affair, was more than two years ago.

PAUL: Two years! Wheeler! That's a long time to live like this.

WHEELER: What do you mean, "like this?"

PAUL: Like a character from a Steely Dan song.

WHEELER: I'm all right. My marriage went south, I'm not the first.

PAUL: How's Gabe?

WHEELER: Who knows? He doesn't talk to me.

PAUL: He doesn't talk to you.

WHEELER: He's thirteen, he doesn't talk to anybody. I don't know what's going on with him. He's all fucked up.

PAUL: Does he talk to Kelly?

WHEELER: He'll give her some sass but that's a whole mother-son thing, I got nothing to do with it. It's them against the world. He just grunts with me. A grunt is a lot, really. You get a grunt, you really feel like you're getting somewhere.

PAUL: But he's all right?

WHEELER: How the fuck would I know?! He could be sniffing glue and pulling the wings off birds, for all I know.

PAUL: Is he still playing ball?

WHEELER: That ended a while ago. He doesn't do anything. He's on the computer a lot.

(A moment.)

PAUL: All right, I should get going.

WHEELER: Yeah, go eat a steak. Tell Margaret I said hello.

PAUL: I'll do it.

WHEELER: And if your friends voted for Trump, tell them a grateful nation says go fuck yourself.

PAUL: All right.

WHEELER: And thanks for your help today, I appreciate it. Y'know, I've got this *hip*.

PAUL: So if we fixed you up, would you be up for that?

WHEELER: Who's we? Is this your idea or is it Margaret's?

PAUL: Margaret's.

WHEELER: Okay, sure, what's the pitch? Who is this?

PAUL: You don't know her.

WHEELER: I like her already.

PAUL: And she's nice looking.

WHEELER: I'm not so hung up on that.

PAUL: I admire that about you. Your lack of standards.

WHEELER: Come on, look at me. You gotta know what pool you're swimming in. Is she roughly my age?

PAUL: She's a little younger than you.

WHEELER: Not too young. I don't want some girl who doesn't remember New Coke.

PAUL: Not too young.

WHEELER: Does she have a job?

PAUL: She has a job. She has a good job.

WHEELER: She's not the mayor or something like that, is she?

PAUL: I don't know if it's a good job. It's an *interesting* job. She's a life coach.

WHEELER: What the fuck.

PAUL: A life coach. She helps people, y'know . . .

WHEELER: What, *breathe*?

PAUL: It's for people who get stuck. They're dissatisfied with life, or some aspect of their life.

WHEELER: Not like anyone *I* know.

PAUL: They procrastinate, or their home life is in a rut, or they just can't decide what it is they really want to do with their life, so they consult with Jules. She's got a healthy business, works for herself, has a lot of clients.

WHEELER: How do you know her?

PAUL: Margaret used her. She helped Margaret launch this new business with the apps.

WHEELER: The carpet thing?

PAUL: Home design. Yes.

WHEELER: How's that going?

PAUL: Going great.

WHEELER: She making any money off that?

PAUL: Not really.

WHEELER: Any?

PAUL: No.

WHEELER: What did you say this woman's name is? Jules?

PAUL: Jules Isch.

WHEELER: Are you saying her first name isn't exactly Jules?

PAUL: No, I'm saying that her last name is Isch. Tell you what, we'll double.

WHEELER: Is that a good idea?

PAUL: It's a great idea. We'll just go out to eat, real casual.

WHEELER: Yeah, nothing fancy, please.

PAUL: Nothing fancy.

WHEELER: Don't take me anywhere that serves *foam*.

PAUL: Burgers and fries, I promise.

WHEELER: C'mon, don't make it like that, that place was over the top.

PAUL: It's a great restaurant.

WHEELER: Dinner should not take six hours. I'm afraid I'm going to wake up and still be eating there. And there was *foam* on my plate! The waiter acted like I should be happy about that. "Excuse me, does someone in the kitchen have rabies?"

PAUL: We'll find someplace you're comfortable. I'll call you.

WHEELER: Thanks, Paul.

(They hug.)

PAUL: Want to play some squash soon?

WHEELER: I got all the time in the world.

PAUL: All right. Enjoy your place.

(Paul exits. Wheeler stares at his apartment.)

SCENE 2

A camera shop.

Wheeler repairs a camera. The shop owner, Michael. Anita performs business with the cash register, etc.

MICHAEL: The best time of my day is when I put my head down on the pillow at night and the worst time of my day is the moment my eyes open in the morning.

WHEELER: Christ, Michael, are you doing anything about that?

MICHAEL: About what?

WHEELER: Your depression.

MICHAEL: I'm not depressed. Maybe it's objective truth. Maybe waking up really *is* the worst moment of my day.

WHEELER: That's not objective. "Worst" is a qualitative judgment. You're ranking the moments of your day and making a judgment that the first moment is the worst.

MICHAEL: I'm the only one experiencing all the moments of my day. I'm the only one qualified to make the judgment.

WHEELER: But that's still not objective truth. Your opinion might be well-informed but it's still just your point of view.

MICHAEL: But there is no other point of view.

WHEELER: That doesn't matter. Just because you're the only person with an opinion doesn't make your opinion objective truth. Anita, please, weigh in on this.

ANITA: I haven't listened to a word you said. And now you made me lose count. What are we talking about?

WHEELER: Say it to her.

MICHAEL: The worst moment of my day is the moment my eyes open in the morning.

ANITA: Sorry to hear that.

MICHAEL *(To Wheeler)*: That's really all I'm looking for.

WHEELER: Fair enough. But morning begins a new day . . . filled with chance, danger, hope. How you look at that is up to you. State of mind. Anita, you feel me? State of mind?

ANITA: State of mind. Don't say "you feel me."

MICHAEL: My mother thinks I'm suicidal. She hides things around the house I could hurt myself with, which is pretty much everything. She hid the fucking cheese grater. I said, "Mother, hiding the cheese grater is not an effective method of suicide prevention."

WHEELER: Traditional cheese grater? Boxy metal thing with little flanged holes in it?

MICHAEL: Yeah. Oh yeah.

WHEELER: How would you go about that, you'd what, you'd—

MICHAEL: I would step on it and flatten it so the holes were running along the edge, and then I would sharply draw that serrated edge across my carotid artery. You open your carotid artery with a gaping wound, you could bleed out in three minutes.

But you can kill yourself with anything, I could kill myself with this fucking pen if I jammed it in my eye,

I could kill myself with this Post-it note. I could kill myself with this money bag. I could kill myself with—

(Cell phone rings.)

Speak of the devil. *(Answers)* Hello, Mother.

(Michael exits.)

WHEELER: Should we be worried about that?

ANITA: I'm not.

WHEELER: Hey, check out this baby: Mamiya/Sekor 2000 DTL. Dinosaur. Good camera. This thing's thirty years old. Shit, it's older than that. It uses something we used to call "film."

ANITA: You came in early to work on that?

WHEELER: I'm not sleeping so good in the new place. I'm scared someone's going to break in and murder me.

ANITA: Who'd want to murder you?

WHEELER: Just, y'know, like drugged-out hippies.

ANITA: Hippies don't murder people.

WHEELER: This is California. They write on the walls in your blood.

ANITA: You're so weird, they have no motivation to murder you.

WHEELER: People with motivation aren't coming after me. People with motivation have no beef with me. I'm not afraid of the tong. I'm afraid of joy killers eating chickpeas out of my skull.

ANITA: How's the pool?

WHEELER: I haven't gotten up the courage yet. The new middle-aged guy hanging around the pool, y'know?

ANITA: Man, if I had a pool, I'd be in there every day.

WHEELER: If I looked like you, I'd be out there too. *(Pause)* That didn't sound right. That's not how I meant it.

ANITA: It's okay.

WHEELER: I mean nobody wants to see me limping around the pool in my shorts, with my bum hip and gray chest hair. I've got middle-age desperation written all over me. I don't mean *now*, I mean that's the reason I haven't gone out to the pool.

ANITA: I get it.

(Michael reenters, now off the phone.)

WHEELER: Everything okay?

MICHAEL: She's off her lithium, so . . . mixed bag. Will you open us up?

(Anita exits.)

Jesus, I could fuck that all night long.

WHEELER: That's doubtful.

MICHAEL: Was I babbling a minute ago? I can't even talk with Anita standing there in that fucking T-shirt. I jerked off last night thinking about those tits and I about hit the ceiling.

WHEELER: You paint a really grisly picture, Michael.

MICHAEL: Was I?

WHEELER: Were you *what*?

MICHAEL: Babbling.

WHEELER: I never know what the hell you're talking about.

MICHAEL: My God, she's not wearing a brassiere.

WHEELER: Yes, she is.

MICHAEL: I think she wants me to take her back in my office and fuck her little pussy.

WHEELER: I haven't seen any indication of that but maybe you're picking up on something I can't see.

(Anita returns.)

MICHAEL: What's your T-shirt say?
ANITA: It's just an old Cal Poly T-shirt.
MICHAEL: "San Luis Obispo." Did you go to college there?
ANITA: Just for a semester.
MICHAEL: You just like the T-shirt?
ANITA: It's worn in.
MICHAEL: You just like the way it feels.

(Weird pause.)

I'm getting a Froyo. Anybody want anything?

(Wheeler and Anita mumble indefinitely. Michael exits.)

WHEELER: You told me you went to UCSD.
ANITA: I did. I also went to Cal Poly. I also went to College of
the Redwoods. I also went to Pepperdine for five minutes.
WHEELER: You studied what again?
ANITA: Liberal arts mash-up. Civics. Religion. *Japanese.*
WHEELER: You going back to school or are you done with it?
ANITA: I've had enough for now.
WHEELER: You know what you'd like to be doing?
ANITA: It changes. Maybe teaching. I may not have the
patience. I'd like to be of service.
WHEELER: Good for you. *(Beat)* That sounded patronizing.
I mean really, good for you, I admire you for that.
ANITA: What about you?
WHEELER: Me, no, I don't want to be of service. Sorry, I just
mean I like my job. I don't like my job. I'm suited for my
job.
ANITA: What'd you do before this?
WHEELER: I was in Chicago, working for the *Sun-Times.*

ANITA: What were you doing?

WHEELER: Taking pictures.

ANITA: I didn't know you took pictures.

WHEELER: I don't. I haven't taken pictures in a long time.

ANITA: Why not?

WHEELER: I'm not very good at it.

(She waits for more.)

My wife and I had a baby and her family's here so I bagged the *Sun-Times* gig and came out. Turned out to be a smart move, since the *Sun-Times* shitcanned all their photographers a few years later cause nobody reads newspapers anymore. Which is weird if you think about it cause if people don't read newspapers anymore, wouldn't it make more sense to shitcan the writers?

ANITA: You didn't answer the question.

WHEELER: I had a gift for documentary portraiture, but my gift was precocious, it didn't develop, as we say in photography. There's enough mediocrity in the world, I didn't need to throw my pictures on the pile. It's not a great mystery. Life is mostly disappointing.

ANITA: State of mind.

WHEELER: State of mind. Christ, it's ten in the morning. This isn't ten-in-the-morning conversation.

ANITA: What time of day does this conversation happen?

WHEELER: Just before dawn. *(Pause)* Want to hit the Lotus Express?

ANITA: I brought my lunch. Trying to save some money.

WHEELER *(Beat)*: You like scallops?

ANITA: I like to eat them.

WHEELER: My virtual friends have a forum on the World Wide Web called Yelp and they inform me there's a new spot in Bay Park with the best scallops in San Diego.

ANITA: Is that so?

WHEELER: Want to give them a try? After work?

ANITA: Ah, I can't, this friend, she's going through a breakup . . .

WHEELER: Oh, oh . . .

ANITA: Yeah, it's not, I just need to spend time with her.

WHEELER: No, yeah, you should. Another night.

ANITA: Yes, definitely.

(They work in silence for a moment.)

No. Not another night. Not another night. I don't have a friend. Sorry, I don't want to lie to you. And I don't want to have to come up with a bunch of excuses for different nights and hope you get the message. We don't need to go through all that, do we?

WHEELER: No, we don't.

ANITA: I don't want to go out with you.

WHEELER: I'm getting that.

ANITA: I don't have to explain why. I don't owe you an explanation.

WHEELER: You don't owe me anything. *(Pause)* It's cause I'm old, right? You're skeeved out cause I'm old.

ANITA: Yes. You're *too old*.

WHEELER: Okay.

ANITA: You're way *too old*.

WHEELER: Okay. I mean I'm not like the Crypt Keeper, am I?

ANITA: Oh my God—

WHEELER: Just tell me, do you think of me like the Crypt Keeper?

ANITA: What is the Crypt Keeper?

WHEELER: Oh, Christ, I'm old.

ANITA: I don't care how old you are, I like you, Wheeler, I really do but . . . you're a mess. And I don't want to be a part of it. That's not a criticism, it's more about timing. I think we take turns blowing our lives up and right now it's your turn. I've been a mess, not that long ago, a lot of shit, a lot of bad decisions, I'm, without going into too much detail, I'm in recovery and it's really tenuous. But I've got it together right now and I'm just trying to keep it together. So let's just be work friends and leave it at that.

(Wheeler nods, turns away.)

And don't be weird with me cause Michael already makes this not the easiest work environment. Maybe don't punish me or give me the silent treatment just because I turned you down.

WHEELER *(Turns to her)*: Thanks for saying "mess" instead of "hot mess," which is a phrase I cannot stand. And more than that, I appreciate you telling me the truth. You're thoughtful.

ANITA: Thanks.

WHEELER: "And he was humiliated."

ANITA: No, come on, it's not like that—

WHEELER: I'm joking, I'm fine, of course we can be friends. We can even have lunch. I'm capable of sitting at the Lotus Express with my friend from work and not mooning at her or crying into my miso soup.

ANITA: You sure about that?

WHEELER: I'll regale you with tales from my disastrous love life. They all end the same way: "And he was humiliated."

SCENE 3

A bar in a restaurant, "Pelican Cove."
   A TV is on, playing a baseball game. Music plays in the restaurant.
   Wheeler stands at a high-top, drinking a beer, eating a burger and fries.
   Minnie, Vietnamese-American, tattooed, rockabilly, stands at another high-top, drinking a beer, putting on makeup.

WHEELER: Big plans?
MINNIE: I was hoping I'd run into some middle-age loser so I could fuck his brains out.
WHEELER *(Pause)*: Then this is your lucky night.

   (Her phone rings, jangling rockabilly. She answers.)

MINNIE: I'm still here. Dude is late. *(Listens)* I have to wait for this guy. *(Listens)* I'm at this heinous restaurant. Want me to prove it to you? *(Listens)* Then get your lame-ass brother to drive down to Chula Vista for your stupid tacos. I have to wait for the manager. *(Listens)* What'd you call me?! Motherfucker, you call me that again, I will scratch your fuckin' eyes out—hello?! *(Hangs up)* Piece of shit.

WHEELER *(Regarding TV commercial)*: Look at *this* prick.

(Minnie seethes, barely takes in the TV.)

This lousy comic book culture we live in, you know? The fanboys who support and demand this shit.

MINNIE: Why's *he* a prick?

WHEELER: *Look* at him.

MINNIE: He just puts on a costume and gets paid.

WHEELER: You make it sound like he doesn't have a choice.

MINNIE: He makes a lot of money.

WHEELER: Al Capone made a lot of money.

MINNIE: Kids like it, it's for kids.

WHEELER: So now all we're supposed to watch is shit made for kids? Fuck your kids. Bunch of allergic autistic mole rats. When I was a kid, movies were made for adults. Kids got *The Apple Dumpling Gang* and we felt lucky to get it. And here's a secret, it's *not* for kids, it's for adult men who can't read. An entire generation of illiterate, infantilized, boy-men.

(Minnie receives a text, reads it.)

I'm kind of a snob. I like old Hollywood movies. *North by Northwest*. *Red River*. *The Hustler*. Foreign movies too, Fellini and Antonioni and Ingmar Bergman. And *Stanley Motherfuckin' Kubrick*. Those guys were genuine artists, they were making shit to last. I can't name any American movies I like that came out after about 1984. What year did *Repo Man* come out? But this garbage, it's all made on computers, they aren't even real people. Even the monsters, used to be your monster was a guy in a rubber suit. He cast a shadow, he bumped into shit, he once actually existed in space and time. I need to see the zipper on his get-up.

(She gives him a withering look.)

I know you don't care. I recognize nobody cares. But I'd still rather say it to you than just, y'know, screaming in the shower.

(She shrugs, yeah, okay, fine.)

You've got a job interview.
MINNIE: Yeah.
WHEELER: You want to work here.
MINNIE: That's why I'm interviewing.
WHEELER: As a waitress.
MINNIE: Hostess.
WHEELER: Hostess.
MINNIE: Yeah.
WHEELER: Is that what you do?
MINNIE: We'll see.
WHEELER: You haven't done it before.
MINNIE: Sh.
WHEELER: Capisce.
MINNIE: Thank you.
WHEELER: What have you been doing?
MINNIE: Shit-work.
WHEELER: What do you want to do?
MINNIE: I want to be a hostess at this restaurant.

WHEELER: What do you want to do with your *life*?

MINNIE: I want to be a hostess at this restaurant.

WHEELER: It's good to have goals.

MINNIE: Fuck you.

WHEELER: You getting sensitive?

MINNIE: Go fuck yourself.

WHEELER: You began this conversation by calling me a loser.

MINNIE: I didn't begin this conversation.

WHEELER: What's your name?

MINNIE: Minnie.

WHEELER: That's good.

MINNIE: You approve.

WHEELER: I'm Wheeler.

MINNIE: Is that your last name?

WHEELER: Everybody calls me Wheeler.

MINNIE: What's your first name?

WHEELER: Dick. Which is why I go by Wheeler.

MINNIE: Oh my God.

WHEELER: What?

MINNIE: We live in the same complex.

WHEELER: Sorry?

MINNIE: I saw you out at the pool. Earlier today.

WHEELER: Ah. Yes. You did.

MINNIE: I knew I'd seen you before. You were hitting on that Mexican girl in the red two-piece.

WHEELER: I was not hitting on her—

MINNIE: I can't believe we live in the same complex, what are the chances of that—?

WHEELER: Kind of slim but it's important you know I was not hitting—

MINNIE: You were totally macking on her, you had on your Speedo—

WHEELER: Not a Speedo actually—

MINNIE: And your big Cuban shirt—

WHEELER: Guayabera, with my rosacea I can't get too much sun—

MINNIE: —and you were drinking a daiquiri—

WHEELER: That was *hers*, not mine—

MINNIE: She's a big girl.

WHEELER: She is, but it's important to me you understand—

MINNIE: She's too much woman for you, Dick.

WHEELER: I won't argue with that but—

MINNIE: What unit are you in?

WHEELER: 217, but it's important to me—

MINNIE: Is that a big one? Two bedroom?

WHEELER: It is a two bedroom.

MINNIE: End unit?

WHEELER: It's important to me you understand I was not hitting on that girl.

MINNIE: Why is that important to you?

WHEELER: Because I am not the kind of guy who goes to the pool in his guayabera and Speedo and drinks a daiquiri and hits on girls.

MINNIE: Aren't you hitting on me?

WHEELER: No.

MINNIE: Then what do you care what kind of guy I think you are?

(Touché.)

Don't sweat it, Dick. You're not my first Rice King *today*.

WHEELER: "Rice King"?

MINNIE: You're a smart guy, you figure it out.

WHEELER: I'm actually not hitting on you, you're way too young for me.

MINNIE: No shit.

WHEELER: How old are you?

MINNIE: Twenty-six and none of your fucking business.

WHEELER: You're older than I thought but you're still too young for me.

MINNIE: Don't you mean you're too old for me?

WHEELER: No, I don't.

MINNIE: How old did you think I was?

WHEELER: I don't know. Younger. You've got that runaway look.

MINNIE: Did you say "runway"?

WHEELER: No, "runaway." Like you ran away. You live with Peanut?

MINNIE: Derek, yeah, and his brother.

WHEELER: Is he the Rice King?

MINNIE: You see him at the pool, why don't you ask him?

WHEELER: I might. You from here?

MINNIE: Yeah.

WHEELER: Born and raised.

MINNIE: Don't say something stupid.

WHEELER: Your parents boat people?

MINNIE: Yeah.

WHEELER: Let me guess, Mom and Dad came over on the boats, married at nineteen, Mom works at a nail salon, Dad's got a garage, no, wait, a *pho shop*. And they're not crazy about your tattoos or your hair and they're really not crazy about punk-ass Derek.

MINNIE: Let *me* guess, you're a deadbeat, work a dead-end job, married, no, wait, *divorced*, hate your wife and kids, hate everybody, depressed, can't get laid, your body's breaking down, the only thing that still runs is your mouth. Not so much fun now, is it?

WHEELER: No, it's not, but you know, actually that's pretty accurate.

MINNIE: God, white people are so sad.

SCENE 4

A karaoke bar. A loud, flat, drunk male voice sings "The Heat Is On."
   Sitting at a table with a pitcher of beer, Wheeler, Paul, Marga-ret, Jules.
   Their voices are pitched loud to be heard over music and bar noise.

JULES *(Cheering on the singer)*: Yeah! "The Heat Is On"!

   (During the following, Jules splits her attention between the table and the unseen singer.)

WHEELER: *Is* it? *Is* the heat on?
PAUL: The heat *is* on for that chap, apparently.
WHEELER: "Chap"?
PAUL: What's your problem with "chap"?

WHEELER: Cor blimey, nowt, guv'nah.	MARGARET: Pip pip cheerio, bumbershoot.

JULES: I love Huey Lewis!

WHEELER: This isn't Huey Lewis, it's— *(To himself)* —never mind, it's all the same, nobody cares.

(Margaret aims an iPhone at the others.)

MARGARET: Okay, you two, picture time. Get out of there, Paul, I don't need a picture of you, I see you every day. Squeeze together, guys. Oh that's nice. One . . . two . . .

WHEELER: Take the picture, Margaret.

MARGARET: Three! Oh that's really sweet! I'll send you a copy.

WHEELER *(To Paul)*: How many Hueys can you name? I've got four.

MARGARET: What kind of beer is this?

PAUL: I've got four.

MARGARET: Is this a lager?

PAUL: Ayinger Celebrator. It's a Doppelbock. Can you believe they have a Doppelbock on tap?!

WHEELER: You have odd enthusiasms.

MARGARET: Don't get me started.

PAUL: What? I like beer.

JULES *(Clinks mugs with Paul)*: I like it too. Woo-hoo!

WHEELER: It's frickin' strong, my eyes are watering . . .

MARGARET: He's threatened to start *making* it.

PAUL: Brewing it. Home brew!

MARGARET: I told him if he let me have another dog, I'd let him make his stupid beer.

PAUL: No, I don't want to go through that again.

WHEELER: What happened to Aubrey?

PAUL: No, no, let's not even get into it, we can't even mention that dog's *name* without a whole—

MARGARET: Oh stop it, don't treat me like that—

PAUL: I'm sorry, did you not *just* experience a meltdown when we stumbled on pictures of Aubrey on the laptop?

MARGARET: That was a bad day and you know it—
WHEELER: I guess I can infer that Aubrey is no longer with us.
PAUL: Aubrey passed away on Valentine's Day.

JULES: That's so sad!   WHEELER: Dogs don't pass away.

MARGARET: Peacefully—
PAUL: Very peacefully. After a long illness. Which is why we were restricted from traveling for, what, the last five years?
MARGARET: Yeah, it was a long time.
PAUL: And I'm not eager to go through that again. We've done it, Aubrey was a great dog.

MARGARET: A *great* dog.   WHEELER: A great dog, yes.

("The Heat Is On" concludes.)

DEEJAY *(Offstage)*: Merle! Thank you, Merle!
MARGARET: Well, that's the deal, the beer for the dog. We both need something to occupy us during the long lonely hours at home.

PAUL: All right—   MARGARET: A lot of couples have offspring to distract them from their shattered dreams.

PAUL: You want to talk about this with *Wheeler* present? Really?
MARGARET: As if you two haven't already had this conversation.
WHEELER: Are you kidding, you guys are my heroes for remaining childless. Everything they say about having kids is true, all the ineffable cosmic shit, but it's also a nightmare and doesn't suit everybody. I think if you guys had a kid, you'd be divorced by now.

DEEJAY *(Offstage)*: Debbie! Debbie from Del Mar!

(Female voice sings "Do You Believe in Magic.")

MARGARET: What makes you say that?

WHEELER: You two would use the kid as barter, or pit the kid against each other. You sure as hell wouldn't put up a united front. Any child from the two of you would be really whacked out.

(An uncomfortable silence. Then:)

MARGARET: That's a shitty thing to say.

WHEELER: Why? I'm complimenting you.

MARGARET: It doesn't sound like a compliment—

PAUL: Yeah, I've never heard a compliment sound like that.

WHEELER: Should I be complimenting you on your parenting skills? You don't have any *kids*.

MARGARET: You should compliment us for recognizing the complexity of having children.

WHEELER: How is that different from what I said?

MARGARET: You make us sound like just this sniping, incompetent couple. You think we're that terrible couple from the cartoons.

WHEELER: I apologize. *Me and Kelly* are the sniping, incompetent couple, and we've got the zombie teenager to prove it. Wait, what terrible couple from the cartoons?

PAUL: Yeah, what terrible couple from the cartoons?

JULES: What are we talking about?

MARGARET: You know, the married couple from the cartoons.

JULES: The Simpsons!

MARGARET: No, not the . . . that awful couple, I can't remember their name.

WHEELER: Well, *think*, this is important to me.

MARGARET: *Why?*

WHEELER: I don't know, it's just the way I'm made.

PAUL: I'm kind of curious myself.

JULES: The Flintstones!

PAUL: The Flintstones weren't awful.

WHEELER: They were a *modern* Stone Age family.

MARGARET: Do not do this to me.

WHEELER: What?! I'm trying to help you think of it.

MARGARET: Purposely distracting me from what I was talking about.

WHEELER: I'm helping you figure out what you were talking about.

MARGARET: Goddamn you,   JULES: The Jetsons!
Wheeler—

WHEELER: Was it the Jetsons? Was it the Flintstones?

PAUL: Blondie and Dagwood?

WHEELER: That was a great marriage, that was a marriage we all envy.

PAUL: He was not very attentive.

WHEELER: *Attentive*, all he did was eat sandwiches and fuck his wife.

PAUL: He fucked his wife in the newspaper?

WHEELER: No, in the pussy.

PAUL: Wow.   MARGARET: Oh boy.

WHEELER: *Boom*, that's right, I said it, and I've got *five* Hueys!

PAUL: Bullshit!

WHEELER: Huey Lewis, Huey Newton, Huey Long, and oddly, two ducks—

PAUL: Two ducks, fuck you!

WHEELER: —one of Donald Duck's nephews and Baby Huey.

MARGARET: You are so weird—

PAUL: What *was* Baby Huey?

WHEELER: An infant duck the size of a man, wearing a diaper. Tragic.

("Do You Believe in Magic" concludes.)

DEEJAY *(Offstage)*: Debbie! Thank you, Debbie!

JULES: Is anyone else going to sing?

WHEELER: I am not a singer so I will not be singing. No one in this bar is a singer! Margaret, don't be mad at me.

MARGARET: You're infuriating.

WHEELER: Just answer one thing. Was it the Flintstones?

PAUL *(Laughing)*: Man, you are really on thin ice, Wheeler . . .

DEEJAY *(Offstage)*: Jules Isch! Jules Isch!

JULES: That's me! I'm up!

(Jules chugs her beer, steps into light on a small stage and sings "Stay." After a verse and a chorus, lights and sound crossfade back to the table.)

WHEELER: If you have even a drop of mercy, kill me now.

MARGARET: I told you.

PAUL: C'mon, you guys were getting on great at the restaurant.

WHEELER: We could talk about the food at the restaurant. The only thing we have in common is that we both eat.

MARGARET: She's a perfectly lovely woman. She's bright, she's personable, she has a lot of energy—

WHEELER: —all true—   MARGARET: —she's young, she
                                   has a cute figure—

WHEELER: Why are you so angry?

MARGARET: Your contrary nature. You can't enjoy anything
unless it's your discovery.

WHEELER: That's inaccurate—

MARGARET: And how dare you say we wouldn't make good parents. How dare you. A lot goes into a choice like that, you
understand? Things you don't know cause they're none
of your business.

WHEELER: Jesus, Margaret, I'm really sorry. I think maybe I'm
drunk from this crazy beer—

MARGARET: I accept your apology. Now if you want to make it
up to us, give this woman a chance.

WHEELER: Margaret—   MARGARET: You don't have to
                                   marry her.

WHEELER: Good, because you know, officially, I'm still married.

MARGARET: Do you see the look on my face?

WHEELER: Doesn't her conviction to this song make you a little
queasy?

MARGARET: No, it doesn't.

PAUL: She's awesome!

MARGARET: She's in the spirit of the evening, give her some
credit. It's a blind date for her too, and she's *trying*. Now
when she comes back, Paul and I are gonna fuck off for a
minute.

WHEELER: No, don't leave me here!

MARGARET: I'm asking you to conduct yourself like a gentleman and make conversation with the nice lady for ten
lousy minutes.

WHEELER: We don't have anything in common, she's not—

MARGARET: *Hush.* Ten minutes. If you can't do it for yourself, then do it for Paul, don't make him look bad for setting this up.

WHEELER: Make *him* look bad, this was *your* idea.

MARGARET *(To Paul)*: You told him this was my idea?!

PAUL: I thought he'd take it seriously if it came from you—

(Margaret stalks off.)

I came so close to pulling this off.

(Paul exits. Jules finishes the song and rejoins Wheeler at the table.)

WHEELER: That was great.

JULES: Thank you kindly.

WHEELER: Great, just great.

JULES: Thanks.

WHEELER: Yes indeedy. Really . . . really great.

JULES: Where did Margaret and Paul go?

WHEELER: Looks like they might be getting ready to sing? Maybe a duet? What do you think they should sing?

JULES: Ooh . . . "Leather and Lace."

WHEELER: Oh my God.

JULES: Are we supposed to drink all this beer?

WHEELER: I don't know that there's an obligation.

DEEJAY *(Offstage)*: La Toya from La Jolla!

(A woman's voice sings a creditable rendition of "How Do I Live?")

JULES: You and Paul go way back.

WHEELER: We went to college together, University of Illinois, me and Paul and Margaret. I went out with Margaret first actually but we sorted all that out a long time ago.

JULES: You all moved out here together?

WHEELER: No, it's coincidence, we had a number of years when we weren't as close but we wound up out here and reconnected.

JULES: That's great. Old friends are the best.

(Wheeler smiles, nods.)

What are you going to sing?

WHEELER: I'm not going to sing. I'm not much of a singer.

JULES: That doesn't matter.

WHEELER: No, I know, clearly, that's the whole idea behind karaoke.

JULES: Right. We're made to sing. People are. It's part of our functionality.

WHEELER: Huh.

JULES: We're designed for certain things. We wouldn't be able to sing if we weren't able to sing. Kind of like flight.

WHEELER: Like flight, I don't follow you.

JULES: We can't fly because we're not designed to fly. We're designed to sing, so we do. We should. We're supposed to, whether we're good at it or not. It's one of the things I encourage a lot of my clients to do, is to sing. It can really open you up. Opens people up.

WHEELER: Really.

JULES: It exposes a lot of vulnerability, singing. You know, we're taught from an early age the things we're good at or not good at so we're screwed up and self-conscious, but also just the *act* of breathing out, sustaining your breath. We can recover old submerged feelings and gain access to our internal selves. We can project so much through song.

WHEELER: I wouldn't've, I wouldn't've . . . I wouldn't've, I wouldn't've thought, thought of that. I don't think like that. You, you say in your work, this is your work as a, a, a, um, a . . .

JULES: Life coach.

WHEELER: Life coach. You, you . . . you coach life.

JULES: Yeah. I mean to the extent that—you know, coaching is, a lot of it is encouragement—

WHEELER: —sure—

JULES: —and motivation? But also a good coach gives people tools and exercises that strengthen their performance.

WHEELER: Right. Wow, maybe I could use some of that cause I—

JULES: I don't know a person alive who couldn't benefit from coaching. *Good* coaching.

WHEELER: Do you study to learn to do that or are you just innately talented at bossing people around?

JULES: No, I studied, I have my degree.

WHEELER: In?

JULES: Happiness.

WHEELER: No, really.

JULES: Really.

WHEELER: No, really though, what is your, you have a degree . . . ?

JULES: I have a master's. In happiness. Come on, sing a song.

WHEELER: No, I really can't, I don't know what I would sing, I—

JULES: "Every Breath You Take."

WHEELER: I hate that song.

JULES: "Piano Man."

WHEELER: I hate that song.

JULES: "Let's Get It Started in Here."

WHEELER: I hate that song. Are you going to name all the songs?

JULES: "Pretty Woman."

WHEELER: I really hate that song. I'm resentful every time I'm stuck somewhere listening to it. How much of my life have I spent forced to listen to that terrible song?

JULES: Elvis.

WHEELER: I hate Elvis.

JULES: Queen.

WHEELER: I hate Queen.

JULES: Maroon Five.

WHEELER: I don't know what that is.

JULES: Radiohead!

WHEELER: Of the many things that could happen tonight, me singing Radiohead is just not on the list. An asteroid will hit this bar before I sing Radiohead.

JULES: You don't like Radiohead?

WHEELER: Until they came along, I'd forgotten music could be so joyless. I will not sing it on a boat, I will not sing it with a goat, I do not like them, Sam-I-am.

JULES: But how can you not like Radiohead?

WHEELER: I do not like so many things and so many of them are things that a lot of people like. I don't like many modern bands really, or old bands, or rock 'n' roll bands, or old or modern rock 'n' roll bands. I like jazz, Miles and Mingus and Art Blakey and Lee Morgan and Coltrane and Herbie Hancock. Everybody digs Bill Evans. Popular music, I don't know . . . I like seventies soul, Stevie Wonder, Steely Dan, I do.

JULES: But *Radiohead*. I mean *Thom Yorke*.

WHEELER: Thom Yorke, that's that scrubby little poser, looks like Martin Short got punched in the eye?

JULES: Come on, he's such a great singer.

WHEELER: Ella Fitzgerald is a great singer.

JULES: It's not just about the notes, it's about his sincerity.

WHEELER: Yeah, sorry, I have to disagree. Because until someone invents a machine that measures sincerity, it's just your perception versus my perception of how sincere someone is. Sincerity can be faked. It's easier to act sincere than it is to perceive insincerity. So you see Thom Yorke as a guy who doesn't need to hit all those pesky notes because he's sincere, whereas I see a guy who is selling a simulation of sincerity so you don't worry about the pesky notes. I think acting sincere is a way to bypass expertise and craftsmanship. And so a real musician who has put in the work but appears less sincere than Thom Yorke might ask, "What did I bother practicing all those years for?" This is like the old Keith Richards argument.

JULES: What old Keith Richards argument?

WHEELER: Well, it's my argument. That he sucks.

("How Do I Live?" concludes.)

DEEJAY *(Offstage)*: Beautiful! Let's hear it for La Toya!

JULES: Are you a musician?

WHEELER: Can't play a note. Just an astute observer of the time in which I live.

JULES: You have a strong point of view. And the ability to articulate it. That's impressive.

WHEELER: Thank you.

JULES: But it's more fun to like things.

(Wheeler can't argue.)

DEEJAY *(Offstage)*: Paul and Margaret! Paul and Margaret!

(They appear on the bandstand.)

WHEELER: Oh, here we go, Steve and Eydie.

JULES: Woo-hoo! "Leather and Lace"!

(Paul and Margaret sing "You Don't Have to Be a Star (To Be in My Show)." After a verse and a chorus, lights and sound crossfade back to the table.)

I don't think I know this one.

WHEELER: Marilyn McCoo and Billy Davis Jr. were members of The 5th Dimension and then they split off and this was their first big hit right out of the gate. It was such a big hit they got their own variety show. When I was a kid if you had a hit song you got your own variety show.

JULES: You know a lot of stuff.

WHEELER: I know nothing of any real value, I'm just old.

JULES: I think you're sweet.

WHEELER: You *do*?!

JULES: I do. You think you're kind of tough. But it's touching that you don't realize how vulnerable you are. You're like a turtle who doesn't know he's lost his shell.

WHEELER: That's . . . actually a very kind thing to say. That, uh . . . yeah.

(She takes his hand.)

But I'm still not singing.

(She laughs, he laughs with her.)

SCENE 5

Wheeler and Jules have sex in Wheeler's bed.

JULES: Oh no you don't understand.

WHEELER: Mm Jesus.

JULES: Oh fuck . . .

WHEELER: Oh God don't . . . don't move.

JULES: Okay. *(Pause)* Why?

WHEELER: I'm about to come.

JULES: So? That's okay.

WHEELER: No, I don't want to.

JULES: Okay. *(Pause)* Why?

WHEELER: Well . . . cause I'm waiting for you.

JULES: No, don't wait for me. Don't wait for me.

WHEELER: Why? I want to wait for you.

JULES: No, don't. It's okay. Come on, go ahead, you can come.

WHEELER: You're sure?

JULES: Yeah, it's fine.

WHEELER: Don't you want to?

JULES: Yeah, but no, it's fine, just do your stuff.

WHEELER: "Do my stuff," c'mon, it's not like that.

JULES: You know what I mean, you're good to go. All clear.

WHEELER: Okay.

JULES: Mm, oh God. Oh God, fuck, no no no, you don't understand.

WHEELER: Jesus.

JULES: Yeah, baby, come on, come in me.

WHEELER: What don't I understand?

JULES: What?

WHEELER: That's the second time you've said I don't understand.

JULES: Don't worry about it.

WHEELER: But what does that mean?

JULES: It doesn't mean anything.

WHEELER: It doesn't?

JULES: Christ, it just feels good, it's just a way of saying it feels good, like, "You don't understand how good this feels."

WHEELER: You seem really turned on.

JULES: That's the idea, right?

WHEELER: Then why don't you want to come?

JULES: Will you just finish, please?

(More activity.)

WHEELER: Oh Jesus my hip . . . !

(He finishes. She soothes him, rubs his back.)

JULES: Yeah, yeah . . . it's okay . . . it's okay . . .

WHEELER: Oh my God . . .

JULES: Shh, there you go . . . it's okay . . .

WHEELER: Jesus . . .

JULES: Shh.

(She rolls away, puts a pillow under her, lies on her stomach, masturbates.)

WHEELER: Hey.
JULES: Mm.
WHEELER: Hey there . . .
JULES: Shh, please . . .
WHEELER: Hey, Jules . . .
JULES: Please don't speak.

(He puts his hand on her back.)

No no, don't.

(He strokes her hair.)

Please don't touch me.

(He watches as she grinds on the bed.)

Goddamn it . . .

(She readjusts, continues masturbating.)

WHEELER: Is there anything I can do—?
JULES: God*damn* it, please, just be quiet.

(She masturbates, frustrated. Wheeler picks up a magazine, begins reading. Jules turns her head, sees him.)

Are you reading the *Atlantic Monthly*?
WHEELER: Yes. Should I leave?
JULES: Goddamn it, Wheeler!
WHEELER: What?

JULES: I was so close!

WHEELER: I'm sorry, it's weird, I don't know what to do!

JULES: Nothing! Can you do that? Nothing?!

WHEELER: Well then what do you even need me for?

JULES: I don't need you for this part! I'm glad you're here, I want you here. But I can only do this part by myself.

WHEELER: Seems like you could do this part by yourself at home, later.

JULES: Jesus, you're an asshole.

WHEELER: What, I do this part by myself all the time!

JULES: We're having sex. Together.

WHEELER: We *were* but then you started your solo career.

JULES: Stop. Please. Think about what you're saying. Because it sounds unloving. Just take a moment and make sure you're saying what you want to say. I don't think you want to say these things. Maybe you're embarrassed or maybe you're just uncomfortable with a woman's sexuality.

WHEELER: Okay, I'm taking a moment. And I know what I want to say.

JULES: Good. What?

WHEELER: *The Lockhorns.*

JULES: What?

WHEELER: Margaret said "cartoon" when she should've said "comic strip." And she was talking about *The Lockhorns*, it was a comic strip by Bill Hoest, just a one-panel gag—

(Jules slaps his face, gets out of bed, puts on underwear.)

Does that mean we're done having sex?

JULES: Quit while you're ahead.

WHEELER: I'm *ahead*?

JULES: I'm vulnerable here. Y'know?

WHEELER: Yeah, okay.

JULES: I have some trouble with my orgasm. It's actually not a big deal, I enjoy sex anyway. A loving partner will take time with me and we can find a good place together. This is our first time in bed. It might've been different with more time, a few weeks.

WHEELER: Jules, I'm sorry.

JULES: Forget it.

WHEELER: No, you're right, I probably got embarrassed and acted like an ass, and I'm really sorry.

JULES: Okay. It's okay, no big deal. I'll . . . I'll get over it.

(Jules moves to the living room, carrying the rest of her clothes.)

WHEELER: Now wait, goddamn it . . .

(Wheeler trails her, pulling the bedsheet around him.)

Stop, just . . . come on, Jules . . . *please stop.*

(She stops.)

C'mon, I was an idiot and you slapped me and I apologized. Can we just talk for a minute?

JULES: I don't know, I'm embarrassed now and I just want to leave.

WHEELER: Well, *don't*, let me make you some eggs or something. I don't have any eggs. I might've seen that in a movie. Let's talk and be nice to each other. Nothing is irrevocable.

(Pause.)

JULES: I'm still drunk.

WHEELER: You kidding, I'm blind. That kraut beer had some kind of wormwood in it. I can't believe my dick even worked. I'm so proud of it, I'm going to write it a thank you note.

JULES: Stop making jokes.

WHEELER: Please don't leave.

JULES: Do you have anything to eat?

(She opens the refrigerator.)

You have a lot of white paper bags.

WHEELER: I've been eating a lot of takeout.

(She closes the fridge, opens a cabinet.)

JULES: Canned beans, canned hearts of palm, canned oysters.

WHEELER: If you ever want to know how pathetic you are, have somebody list the contents of your pantry.

JULES: Here we go, score. Girl Scout cookies.

WHEELER: Thank Christ. I knew when I bought them, "Good karma, this will come back to me."

(She opens the box, eats cookies.)

JULES: *Atlantic Monthly.* You jerk.

(He caresses her. She walks around, takes in the apartment.)

I don't really know where we are.

WHEELER: Linda Vista.

JULES: Did we walk by a pool? Am I imagining that?

WHEELER: Yeah, there's a pool.

JULES: This place is okay.

WHEELER: It's got a 1980s East Berlin vibe . . . but it's never looked better than right now.

JULES: Why?

WHEELER: Because you're walking around it in your underwear. Why are you single? It doesn't make sense to me.

JULES: I got hurt.

WHEELER: Bad?

JULES: Pretty bad. It's taken me a long time to get back.

WHEELER: Are you back?

JULES: No. I'm getting there.

WHEELER: How will you know when you get there? I feel like I won't know I got back until I start back down.

JULES: You have to learn to love the place you are. *(Beat)* You think Paul and Margaret will be surprised we had sex?

WHEELER: Yes.

JULES: Why?

WHEELER: They probably assume you have more sense.

JULES: Let's not tell them.

WHEELER: Okay.

JULES: I'm totally telling them. What did they tell you about me?

WHEELER: Only good things. All of them true. What did they tell you about me?

JULES: That you were broken and joyless, without prospects and past your prime.

WHEELER *(Laughs heartily)*: They know me even better than I thought they did.

JULES: Margaret said you were very smart and had a good sense of humor. And that you were tall and handsome.

WHEELER: That's not all she said.

JULES: She told me about your divorce. She didn't go into detail. She said it was messy. She mentioned you're an amazing photographer.

WHEELER: Former photographer.

JULES: This is one of yours?

(She pulls a framed photograph from a still-not-emptied moving box. She holds it, studies it.)

It's stunning.

WHEELER: It's all right.

JULES: It's a lot better than all right. Is this your boy?

WHEELER: That's a little girl actually. My wife Kelly and I went to Greece on our honeymoon. And while we were there, Kelly got dysentery and had to be hospitalized for a couple of days. I went to find the coffee shop and got lost in the hospital and I wound up in a children's ward. I was standing at the end of a long aisle between rows of hospital beds with sick children. And at the other end of the aisle I saw this little girl, a patient. She saw me, and broke into a huge smile, and went into a dead run, right for me. *(Chokes up)* And I bent down and she threw her arms open and I opened my arms and scooped her up and held her. There's no explanation for it, we didn't talk. Nurse came and took her from me and I took that picture. Sorry, I didn't mean to get emotional. I guess I really am still drunk. *(Pause)* That's too easy. I've been sad for a while . . . and I feel good with you.

JULES: I want to see you again.

WHEELER: Good. I want to see you too.

JULES: Yes?

WHEELER: Yes. Yes. I like you, Jules . . .

(They kiss. They heat up, move back to the bedroom. The doorbell chimes.)

Fucking *hippies.*

(Wheeler approaches the door.)

JULES: Hold on, wait for me to . . .

(Jules returns to the bedroom. Wheeler opens the door.
   Minnie stands outside, holding a laundry basket heaped with
her stuff.)

MINNIE: Remember me?
WHEELER: Yeah, of course, Minnie, what's going on?
MINNIE: Can I come in?
WHEELER: Yeah, come in.

(She steps into the apartment. Wheeler checks outside, closes the
door, secures the sheet around him.)

MINNIE: My boyfriend and I got in a fight and he hit me and
   took off and I don't have anywhere to go.
WHEELER: Let's call the cops.
MINNIE: No, don't, it'll just make things worse.
WHEELER: He hit you, we have to call the police. We should
   get you to a hospital and make out a report—
MINNIE: Please don't do that. Don't call the cops, they won't
   find him anyway, he took off, he's going up to Vancouver.
WHEELER: Where did he hit you?
MINNIE: In the stomach. I might be pregnant. He hit me in
   the stomach.

(Minnie, stoic to this point, sobs.)

WHEELER: It's okay. It's okay.
MINNIE: I don't have anywhere to go. We were staying with his
   brother, in his brother's place, and he hates me. I would
   stay with my friend Gina but she doesn't have room

and my friend Dre lives with these junkies and it's a bad
scene—

WHEELER: What about your parents, can you—?

MINNIE: They threw me out.

WHEELER: It's okay, you can stay here tonight.

MINNIE: Are you sure?

WHEELER: It's fine, I've got the extra bedroom.

MINNIE: I was really scared. If you hadn't been here, I thought
I'd have to go sleep in the park or something.

WHEELER: No one's sleeping in the park. We'll get it all figured
out.

(Jules, now fully clothed, enters from the bedroom.)

This is my friend Minnie. She's going to stay here for a
while.

Act Two

SCENE 1

Wheeler's apartment.

Wheeler, Jules, and Minnie watch Barry Lyndon. *Schubert, Trio in E-flat major, op. 100. Dry Michael Hordern narration. Pizza boxes, beer bottles.*

Wheeler realizes both women are dozing. He stops the film.

WHEELER: All right, never mind.

JULES: What?! I'm watching!

WHEELER: You're sleeping.

JULES: I'm totally watching the movie!

WHEELER: You're *snoring*.

JULES: I'm *breathing*.

MINNIE: *I'm* sleeping, cause it's fucking boring.

WHEELER: I warned you it's slow. It demands a 1975 attention
    span.

MINNIE: It's been on for about eight hours.

WHEELER: As soon as I put it on, I thought, "*Barry Lyndon* is not the best Kubrick movie you could lead with." I should've started you out on *Dr. Strangelove* or even *Full Metal Jacket*.

MINNIE: Good plan, Vietnamese girls love *Full Metal Jacket*.

JULES: I'm sorry, I had an early morning.

WHEELER: Stop apologizing to me.

JULES: It was just a pizza coma, I'm awake now, start from the intermission.

MINNIE: You know your movie's too long when you have to take an intermission. Don't get me wrong, that was my favorite part.

JULES: It's so beautiful, the photography and the costumes.

WHEELER: Thank you. Minnie, did you like the pretty pictures?

MINNIE: Who cares? That guy is a douche rocket.

JULES: His opportunism is complex, right? At that time, rising in the social ranks just wasn't possible.

MINNIE: I really don't care about that. This pizza is fucking soggy.

JULES (*To Wheeler*): Don't you think so? Why do you like it so much?

WHEELER: Y'know, to be honest, I might be with Minnie on this, I haven't seen it in a long time and I'm sitting here thinking, "What the hell is this movie about?"

MINNIE: It's fucking boring. Movies are boring, they're all so fake. Actors look so stupid when they're crying and screaming at each other. Why should I care about somebody else's phony story? God, this pizza is making me sick.

JULES: We project our own lives onto the story. We think about how we might behave in a set of circumstances.

MINNIE: That's so great that you pretend you're English aristocrats from another century but I don't actually see myself as any of these people. And I don't want to. And

I don't think that's why this man made this movie. I think he was just showing off.

Oooo, look out, people, I need to take a dump.

WHEELER: Nice.

(Minnie grabs a magazine, exits.)

JULES: Sorry I closed my eyes, we just can't start movies after—

WHEELER: Please, *please* stop apologizing to me.

JULES: Sorry, it's a holdover from my last boyfriend, he had a way of making me feel like I was always screwing up.

WHEELER: That guy was a knob.

JULES: He was a dumb boy. I got me a *man* now.

(They kiss.)

I really wanted to fool around tonight.

WHEELER: Why didn't you say so? I would've come to your place.

JULES: We should've, we could've gotten into my big bathtub.

WHEELER: I have to say, I am not a fan of doing it in the bathtub.

JULES: It's romantic!

WHEELER: It has some practical difficulties. I'm not a fan of fucking in the tub or the shower or the pool or the ocean. Or water, I could've just said water.

JULES: Why?

WHEELER: It's too squeaky. It's like trying to fuck a balloon.

(More kissing.)

JULES: You made a very good impression on my dad.

WHEELER: We bonded over our hatred of the phrase, "No worries."

JULES: Just you being in love with his daughter did the trick.

(Minnie enters.)

MINNIE: Don't go in there.

WHEELER: Man, you're fast.

MINNIE: It's an Asian thing.

WHEELER: Really?

MINNIE: No.

JULES: Okay. I should get going.

WHEELER: You're not spending the night?

JULES: I have a client in the morning. Walk me outside? Night, Minnie.

MINNIE: Good night.

WHEELER *(To Minnie)*: I'll be right back. I got that ice cream you like.

(Wheeler walks Jules outside.)

Are you mad about something?

JULES: What? No, I don't like poop talk. Are you supporting her?

WHEELER: I'm picking up the grocery tab.

JULES: Has she seen a doctor?

WHEELER: I don't pry.

JULES: Make her go.

WHEELER: I can't make her go.

JULES: I'll pay for it, okay? But she needs to see someone. She's not taking care of herself.

WHEELER: Okay, I'll get into it.

JULES: What does your week look like?

WHEELER: Work, followed by dinner, followed by distracting myself from wondering how I screwed up my life.

JULES: Hey pal, you've been with *me* every night for—

WHEELER: Sorry, sorry, it's a holdover from my last boyfriend.

JULES: Want to have dinner with me Thursday?

WHEELER: Why should Thursday be different from every other night?

JULES: Cause Thursday is our one-month anniversary.

WHEELER: Oh Jesus, are we doing that?

JULES: One month is auspicious.

WHEELER: I hate auspice. If we do anniversaries by the month, I'm always going to forget, or not get a present, or get—

JULES: I don't need a present. And we're done after this one.

WHEELER: Really, this one's the last?

JULES: Are you free on Thursday?

WHEELER: I'm a camera repairman. I've got nothing forever.

JULES: You know I don't like it when you say that.

WHEELER: It's so completely true.

JULES: You have a higher calling.

WHEELER: Is Jesus coming for a visit?

JULES: I've seen your pictures, babe.

WHEELER: You've seen maybe five photographs out of the tens of thousands I've taken—

JULES: You have a unique talent, you capture something essential—

WHEELER: You don't know what you're talking about.

JULES: Let's just agree to disagree.

WHEELER: No, let's just disagree.

JULES: I'm only trying to encourage you.

WHEELER: There's a hint of expectation though, like I'll emerge from the cocoon a beautiful butterfly. This is it for me. I'll die a caterpillar.

JULES: Maybe you'll die as my caterpillar.

WHEELER: That's a little creepy but I know what you were going for.

(They kiss.)

JULES: I love you, Wheeler.

WHEELER: Love you too, kid. I'll walk you to your car.

JULES: I got the good spot, I'm right there. I'll text you.

WHEELER: I'll text you back.

(*She exits. Wheeler watches until she's safe, waves.*
He heads inside. Minnie is drinking Jack Daniel's, watch-ing Barry Lyndon.)

Pour me a shot.

(*She does.*)

MINNIE: Why didn't Jules stay the night?

WHEELER: She has to get up early.

MINNIE: It's not cause of me, is it?

WHEELER: Have you been to a doctor?

MINNIE: Sure.

WHEELER: You have?

MINNIE: I went a couple weeks ago.

WHEELER: You did?

MINNIE: You gonna keep doing that?

WHEELER: You didn't tell me you were going.

MINNIE: Sorry, *Dad*.

WHEELER: What did he say?

MINNIE: *She* said I was about eight weeks.

WHEELER: Pregnant?

MINNIE: No, eight weeks old. Yes, pregnant.

(*He takes the whiskey away from her.*)

Hey.

WHEELER: You're not getting wasted in my house.

MINNIE: I'm not getting wasted, I'm having a drink. And this isn't a house, it's an apartment.

WHEELER: It's *my* house, in the sense of home. If you play word games with me, you're going to lose. You have to take care of yourself if you're going to stay here.

MINNIE: I'm not keeping it. Do I get a sermon now?

WHEELER: You get no sermon from me, I think a woman should be able to terminate until the child can make a cogent argument in its own defense. I'm still not comfortable with you drinking in your condition.

MINNIE: I wouldn't want to make you uncomfortable.

WHEELER: Did he say the child was healthy?

MINNIE: She.

WHEELER: Did she say the child was healthy?

MINNIE: It's not a child.

WHEELER: Did she say the fetus was healthy?

MINNIE: What do you care?

WHEELER: This Thursday it'll be a month you've been staying here. I feel some responsibility.

MINNIE: You have no responsibility.

WHEELER: Get an abortion and you can drink all you want.

MINNIE: That would make a kick-ass bumper sticker.

WHEELER: Does Derek know you're pregnant?

MINNIE: I'm trying to watch this sad ginger motherfucker.

WHEELER: Have you heard from Derek?

MINNIE: No.

WHEELER: You run into his brother?

MINNIE: I've seen him. We don't talk.

WHEELER: Gimme the nod, I'll walk down there and punch his ticket.

MINNIE: He would destroy you.

WHEELER: No, he wouldn't. You taking anything, vitamins or anything?

MINNIE: Fuck this, I'm going to bed.

WHEELER: When are you doing it, the abortion?

MINNIE: Good night.

(She retreats. He pursues.)

WHEELER: When?

MINNIE: What difference does it make?

WHEELER: Let me take you.

MINNIE: No.

WHEELER: You should have someone with you.

MINNIE: Who cares if you're with me or I'm alone. I don't care about it and I don't want to talk about it. It's all the same, it's all just pointless and stupid.

WHEELER: Let me take you.

MINNIE: Okay.

(Wheeler kisses Minnie. She returns the kiss.)

SCENE 2

Wheeler and Minnie have sex in Wheeler's bedroom.

WHEELER: You don't understand! You don't understand!
MINNIE: Don't stop, fucker! I'm almost . . .

(They groan, finish. Wheeler collapses.)

You okay, big fella?
WHEELER: No, I'm not. I'm not okay. I'm fifty years old.
MINNIE: You do all right.
WHEELER: I haven't had that much exercise since about five
    years ago, when I got chased by a dog. I don't know if my
    heart can take it. Or my hip. Or my brain, I'm having sen-
    sory overload. It's like the trip scene from *2001: A Space
    Odyssey*. It's okay, I know you don't get the reference, that's
    part of your charm. What time is it, we've been fucking
    for hours.

MINNIE: What is it with you and *time*?
WHEELER: I'm *fifty*.

(He strokes her, studies her.)

Oh my God, you're . . . unexpected.
MINNIE: I didn't expect to fuck the old dude in the Speedo.
WHEELER: You like me?
MINNIE: Sure. You're a weirdo. I like weirdos.
WHEELER: I didn't let you stay here cause there was something
    in it for me. I mean, look, I'm. I'm capable of every kind
    of bad behavior known to man.
MINNIE: You don't have to go through a whole thing here—
WHEELER: I haven't been watching you, I haven't been schem-
    ing, waiting for my moment. I'm as surprised as you are.
MINNIE: I'm not gonna make trouble for you, Dick.
WHEELER: I didn't think you were.
MINNIE: Then what are you talking about?
WHEELER: You *move* me.

(Pause.)

MINNIE: I want some ice cream.

(She begins to put on her clothes.)

WHEELER: What's going on, are you okay?
MINNIE: I just want ice cream.

(She dresses in silence.)

WHEELER: What?
MINNIE: I'm pregnant and I don't have any money and I don't
    have a place to live. So making you feel less guilty about
    cheating on your girlfriend is not my priority.

WHEELER: I don't feel guilty.

MINNIE: If you convince yourself this is more than chemical you get to feel like a good guy again. That's all guys like you care about, telling yourself what a good guy you are.

WHEELER: I like you, Minnie. I'm trying to tell you, I like your way, *you*, I like *you*, the way you think and talk. And look and taste. I look at you, I get that ache. Actual heartache.

MINNIE: Wake up, Dick. Life looks kinda sweet here with a pretty girl in your bed. In the moonlight. In Linda Vista. But this is not your wet dream. And I'm not a doll, I'm not a sweet Asian flower.

WHEELER: I don't think you're a—

MINNIE: In fact, I'm no prize. I make my way on my own and every relationship I've ever had, I've set on fire.

WHEELER: We've got a lot in common.

MINNIE: You're not listening to me. I'm making a promise and you need to listen. I promise . . . I'll hurt you. It's what I do.

SCENE 3

Wheeler and Paul get dressed in a locker room after squash.

WHEELER: "I am making a promise and you need to listen to me. I *promise* I'll hurt you."

PAUL: She said that? What is that? It's like the Curse of the Pharaohs.

WHEELER: Paul, she's so fantastic, she's dark and funny and smart, and she sees through all the phony bullshit, she completely ruined *Barry Lyndon* for me. And the sex— We don't talk about sex, right? You and me.

PAUL: Are we going to talk about sex? Let me put some pants on.

WHEELER: I won't be graphic.

PAUL: I've been married twenty-six years, I'm begging for graphic.

WHEELER: I felt *changed*. I was *changed* by the sex.

PAUL: Your success with women baffles me. You made them watch *Barry Lyndon* and you still got laid, how do you

66

get away with that? And how are you still beating me at squash, you need a hip replacement. It's humiliating.

WHEELER: I feel pretty sick about Jules.

PAUL: Sure. Not sick enough to *not* fuck the twenty-year-old Vietnamese rockabilly girl, but what're you gonna do?

WHEELER: What *am* I gonna do?

PAUL: What. Are you asking for my advice?

WHEELER: Yeah. You're my *friend*.

PAUL: You've never asked my advice before.

WHEELER: I never needed it before.

PAUL: Debatable. What are you asking *about*, specifically?

WHEELER: I know what a great lady Jules is, I'm not a fool. But Minnie provokes something protective in me. I have *thoughts*. About the future.

PAUL: A potential future with the twenty-year-old rockabilly girl.

WHEELER: *Pregnant* rockabilly girl. The baby is a factor.

PAUL: It is? You want to have a baby?

WHEELER: I might. Paul, I may be in love.

(Paul thinks.)

PAUL: My advice is: You're going to do what you're going to do.

WHEELER *(Pause)*: Wait, that's your advice? That's not advice.

PAUL: It is. That's my advice. "You're going to do what you're going to do."

WHEELER: That's a prediction. That's not *even* a prediction, of course I'm going to do what I'm going to do.

PAUL: Exactly.

WHEELER: I can't do anything *other* than what I'm going to do.

PAUL: Right.

WHEELER: So how is that advice?

PAUL: It's the best advice. It's the truth.

WHEELER: It can't be anything *but* the truth. But what it doesn't tell me is what I *should* do.

PAUL: What difference does that make?

WHEELER: Huh?

PAUL: What you *should* do has nothing to do with what you *will* do.

WHEELER: Shouldn't it?

PAUL: Probably.

WHEELER: Walk me through it.

PAUL: Let's say what you should do is find some way to help Minnie with her problems and move her out of your apartment. Ask Jules to marry you and live happily ever after.

WHEELER: This is a hypothetical.

PAUL: Yeah, I'm not saying that's what you *should* do. I'm saying let's say I *say* that's what you should do. Does that mean that's what you're going to do? No. Because you're going to do what you're going to do. That's what I'm saying.

WHEELER: But what *should* I do?

PAUL: It doesn't matter.

WHEELER: How can you say it doesn't matter?! That's all that matters!

PAUL: No, it isn't. No, it isn't. In fact, the only thing that matters is what you're *going* to do. Because that's what you're going to *do*. *(Beat)* Helpful?

WHEELER: No, it's not helpful. At all. It's really *un*helpful. It's like saying . . . it's like not saying anything! You didn't say anything!

PAUL: I said the truth.

WHEELER: You think I should marry Jules.

PAUL: I didn't say that.

WHEELER: But that's what you think.

PAUL: I do not think that.

WHEELER: You *don't* think I should marry Jules.

PAUL: I don't think that either. I think that if you marry Jules, then that's the thing you will have done.

(Wheeler is speechless.)

Margaret and I went out with some friends the other night.

WHEELER: Are you changing the subject?

PAUL: Not really, just a different approach. Maybe I am. I don't know. Just listen: So Margaret and I went out with friends the other night, married couple, about our age.

WHEELER: Do I know these people?

PAUL: No, no, these are . . . legitimate people. And the subject turned to marriage and . . . marriage. How hard it is, marriage, what a rotten deal, it's for suckers, right, all that jazz. Then the guy reached over and took his wife's hand and said, "Y'know, even though marriage is so hard and has its ups and downs," blah-blah, "all in all, on the *balance*, on the *whole*, I can't imagine my life without her and it's been great . . ." I don't remember it all but, "It was worth it." He said that, "It's been worth it." And I looked at Margaret. And it was a poignant moment really, because I looked at Margaret and I couldn't say it. And *Margaret* couldn't say it either. Cause—and this is unspoken and will always remain unspoken—all in all, on the *balance*, on the *whole*, it's maybe *not* worth it. Maybe it's just really not worth it.

(Pause. Wheeler stares at him.)

You've been married. Do you disagree?

WHEELER: My marriage is past tense. *My* marriage wasn't worth it.

PAUL: I'm *happily* married, present tense, and I'm telling you it's not worth it. And I really am happily married. I love my wife. I love her and respect her and I don't want to give the impression that I live in regret because I don't. *I did what I was going to do.* But I can't say what I should have done. Because I don't know.

WHEELER: Okay. I follow you.

PAUL: Gun to her head, Margaret would say the same thing.

WHEELER: Yeah. Y'know, when people are actually holding a gun to your head, I don't think they ask questions like that, like, "Was it worth it, marrying Paul?"

PAUL: No, right, usually it's more like, "Where's the safe?"

WHEELER: "Get your fucking ass back in that walk-in freezer."

(They resume getting dressed.)

But *now.* As we advance into our dotage . . . ?

PAUL: Is it a comfort to have someone with me? For illness and the death of parents and the inevitable tightening of our social circle? Is it a comfort? Of course. But you're a smart guy, Wheeler, you know there's a price to pay for living your life the way you do. There's also a price to pay for living life the way *I* do. Nobody gets out of this for free.

WHEELER: But when you're on your deathbed, you'll have Margaret to—

PAUL: I have had it with the deathbed. We burn a lot of fuel thinking about the deathbed. How long do you plan to spend on your deathbed? A day, a week? Maybe a couple months, at most. You got a whole lifetime before you get to the deathbed. Maybe live your life the way you want and just accept that the deathbed is not going to be the high point. You're all alone on your deathbed? Cheer up, you're about to die.

(Pause.)

WHEELER: So you're saying *don't* marry Jules.

PAUL: I'm saying . . .

WHEELER: I'm going to do what I'm going to do.

PAUL: Grab whatever happiness you can. Whether it's a day or a week. You don't know what's gonna happen. You'll fuck it up, whatever you do. Maybe Minnie promised she'd hurt you because she's smart enough to know it's all gonna get fucked up *regardless*. Cause no matter what you do, we'll all be on the deathbed eventually, whether we have company or not.

Don't tell my wife about this conversation.

SCENE 4

Wheeler and Jules have dinner. She hands him a gift box.

WHEELER: We said no presents.

JULES: No, I said I didn't need a present. And I don't.

WHEELER: How's that supposed to make me feel?

JULES: Cared for. Just open it, it's really no big thing.

> *(He opens the gift box, revealing a picture frame.)*

WHEELER: Aspirational gifts? You're not my mom.

JULES: No, it's not the frame, it's—

WHEELER: Let me explain this, once and for all, then let's close
   the subject. Kelly and I moved out here and I *exhibited*, put
   some photos in a gallery, some bullshit *theme*, wine and
   cheese, whatever the fuck, and the needle didn't move.
   Nobody came, I didn't sell anything, and I received exactly
   one review that called my photos "revealing and surprising."

JULES: Isn't that good? That's—

WHEELER: He was *wrong*. It's what I've been telling you and you just won't listen, I'm no good. What do you think photography is, anyway? Do you know? What do you think it is?

JULES: What it is? You're asking me what photography is?

WHEELER: You want to talk about it, let's talk about it. What is photography?

JULES: It's. Okay, bear with me, this feels like a test. It's a universal language. Because we all respond to . . . a moment captured in time. A photograph provides a way for us to see who we are, a sort of . . . visual poem. You're just waiting for me to finish saying stupid things so you can tell me what it really is.

WHEELER: A photograph is light.

JULES: Okay.

WHEELER: That's all it is. It's light. If you can express a personal vision by the capture of light, you're an artist. If you can't, you're just another asshole pushing a button on your phone a hundred times a day. And please believe me when I tell you I am just another asshole.

JULES: Think it's possible you're a little hard on yourself?

WHEELER: There is such a thing as expertise. I would have been so grateful if that critic had seen how shallow my photos are. I would be so grateful for some genuine critical thinking, for a call to account. Bob Dylan wins the Nobel Prize for Literature; I made a fried egg sandwich this morning, I'm up for a James Beard Award.

JULES: Your standards are unreasonably high—

WHEELER: My standards are right in the pocket, baby. The erosion of the standards of the general public—educational, intellectual, social, ethical standards—have so inured us to hype we turn reality TV stars into heads of state.

JULES: So you think there's some correlation between Trump and you getting a favorable review?

WHEELER: Yes. It's called integrity.

JULES: Take a moment and think about something you have positive associations with.

WHEELER: I could have a positive association with another drink. What was the waitress's name? Lane, Park . . . Boulevard?

JULES: Jesus, you are on fire tonight.

WHEELER: I think we should stop seeing each other.

JULES: What?

WHEELER: Yeah. I don't want to see you anymore.

JULES: Are you serious?

WHEELER: I don't think we're a good fit. In a lot of ways. You don't listen to me.

JULES: I listen to you.

WHEELER: I think we should stop this before we get too far into it.

JULES: You didn't even look at the picture. The gift isn't the frame, it's the picture. Margaret took it on our first date, that night at karaoke.

WHEELER: I'm . . . I'm sorry, I didn't see the picture.

JULES: I don't think we should break up. We're good together.

WHEELER: We're not. We are not good together. Because you have all this positivity and forward momentum and I'm not built like that. And it's not the right timing, with my divorce, and Gabe is having trouble, I shouldn't—

JULES: Don't use Kelly and Gabe as an excuse. You don't have anything to do with them. You don't even see Gabe. You've hardly seen him since we started—

WHEELER: You do not even know what the fuck you are talking about. If any of that is your business. And it isn't. You don't know what I'm going through with my wife and my child.

JULES: I asked to meet him and you wouldn't—

WHEELER: My God, Jules, my *child.*

JULES: Can we please take some time and talk about this—?

WHEELER: You want to lecture me about raising children? How dare you.

JULES: You won't even let me talk! You won't even listen to me—!

WHEELER: You're hysterical.

JULES: I'm not hysterical, I'm upset. You're breaking up with me because I gave you a picture of us together.

WHEELER: Not just that, a lot of things.

JULES: Like what? Please explain this to me because I'm reeling.

WHEELER: Like this positive attitude I just—see, you're not even listening to me *now*, I tell you why and you don't even—

JULES: You like that about me, you like that I've brought some light and some energy into your life. You told me you did.

WHEELER: It doesn't make me feel good to be with someone so much better than me.

JULES: We've been falling in love. I'm not wrong about that. I know how that feels. That's real. Why are you doing this? Are you seeing someone else?

WHEELER: No.

JULES: You can tell me.

WHEELER: No, I'm not.

JULES: You can, you know, we never said we couldn't see other people, so if you've seen someone else, I won't be upset.

WHEELER: I'm not seeing anyone else. I haven't seen anybody else.

JULES: Really?

WHEELER: Really.

JULES: Really.

WHEELER: Yes. Really. No, I have not seen anybody else.

JULES: So it's just me, you just hate me, all of the sudden—

WHEELER: I don't—please. I don't hate you, I think you're amazing.

JULES: What have I done wrong?

WHEELER: No, God, look, you haven't done anything, I told you, I'm a son of a bitch, I'm a misanthropic piece of shit, I should be taken out into a field and shot in the back of the head, I'm a terrible person—

JULES: —no you're not—

WHEELER: —I'm just a fucking pile of rotting garbage and I deserve all the worst things in life—

JULES: —no, don't say those things . . .

(She weeps.)

WHEELER: Do you ever worry the waitress just quit, just decided she didn't want to wait tables anymore and walked out the back door? How long would it take them to figure it out and bring me another drink?

(She continues to weep.)

No, really, I'm a real piece of shit.

SCENE 5

Wheeler, Minnie, Paul, and Margaret have a picnic in Balboa Park.
Minnie is twenty-eight weeks pregnant.

MINNIE: We've got a list of maybe twenty names but some of them are jokes really. "Horton Heat," and what was the lightning one?

WHEELER: "Kid Lightning." That's your middleweight champ right there.

PAUL: Is "Wheeler" on the list?

MINNIE: I think Wheeler ends with Wheeler.

PAUL: Gabe could still use it—

MARGARET: What about the baby's *last* name? Will his last name be Wheeler?

MINNIE: I'd feel weird forcing a name on a kid that's not his biological father's.

MARGARET: Everything that happens to a baby is forced on him. Babies don't make choices. What's your full name?

MINNIE: Minnie Tran.

MARGARET: I mean your real name. Is your real name Minnie?

MINNIE *(Pause)*: Trần Biến.

MARGARET: Trần's your family name.

MINNIE: Right.

WHEELER: I didn't know that.

MARGARET: You probably didn't ask.

WHEELER: Folks? I have to tell you the truth: I love pineapple.

MARGARET *(To Paul)*: Pour me some more wine, please.

WHEELER: No champagne?

MARGARET: No thanks.

WHEELER: What about Paul's tasty home brew, aren't you obligated?

PAUL: She doesn't like it.

MARGARET: I can't handle it, I got drunk on my ass the first batch he made.

PAUL: She did, she turned into Courtney Love.

MINNIE: I'd like to see that.

MARGARET: No, you wouldn't.	PAUL AND WHEELER: No, you would not.

WHEELER: I like it. It's malty.

PAUL: I'm still playing with the formula but—

(Minnie gasps, holds her belly.)

MINNIE: Man, he is kicking today.

WHEELER: He wants to be outside on this beautiful day. Isn't it amazing? Another gorgeous day in sunny Southern California.

PAUL: What are you saying? Who *are* you?

(She gasps again.)

WHEELER *(Feels her belly)*: He's going for it, isn't he?

MINNIE: You guys want to feel?

MARGARET: No.

PAUL: Sure, do you mind? *(Feels Minnie's stomach)* That's great.

MINNIE: I shouldn't be weirded out by it but I am a little. I feel like I should be on Animal Planet.

MARGARET *(Laughs)*: I was here watching *Romeo and Juliet* one night last summer, right over there, and during the balcony scene, we all became aware of this horrible smell, like burning hair. And it got worse and worse, bad enough to make you gag, and you could tell the actors were smelling it too, the looks on their faces. Finally my girlfriend and I just had to leave, it was too disgusting. Turns out— the zoo is right behind the stage of course—turns out one night every summer, they cremate all the dead animals. We were all sitting there breathing this exotic barbecue. *(Laughs, then to Minnie)* Do you like the Shakespeare they do here in the park?

MINNIE: I've never been.

MARGARET: Oh you should go. They do a great job. Don't wait for Wheeler to take you, I'm sure it's not good enough for him. Too bougie or something.

WHEELER: Something like that.

MARGARET: What do you guys do for fun?

MINNIE: We've been getting out to hear a lot of music.

WHEELER: Rockabilly's a lot of things but bougie isn't one of them.

PAUL: Yeah, seems like you've gone all in on this new Daddy-O thing. All the way down to your brothel creepers.

MARGARET: What?

WHEELER: Creepers, my shoes.

MARGARET: But what did you call them?

PAUL: Brothel creepers, essential for any serious rockabilly fan.

MINNIE *(Correcting)*: Greaser. Betties and greasers.

WHEELER: I'm impressed you know that.

MARGARET: Come on, you're both masters of the inane. But I never realized you were a slave to fashion. Next thing you know you're going to have a tattoo.

(A beat.)

PAUL: You didn't.

(Minnie whacks Wheeler. He rolls up his sleeve, shows them a tattoo on his arm.)

Oh my God. A *heart*?!

MARGARET: Look, Paul, your friend Wheeler has a picture of a heart on his arm.

MINNIE: And it has a little ribbon around it that says, "Minnie."

PAUL: Who *is* this tattooed pineapple-lovin' motherfucker?

WHEELER: Sometimes the universe spins you in unexpected directions.

MINNIE: He cried like a girl.

WHEELER: It fucking hurt!

MINNIE: The things we do for love . . .

(Wheeler and Minnie make out.)

MARGARET *(Faux touched)*: Aww, y'know, that's really very stupid.

PAUL: Really though, a fucking *heart*?

MARGARET: Don't you see he's in love, he wears his heart on his sleeve. Wheeler's shouting from the rooftops, "Look, I have a heart!"

PAUL: She's not right, is she?

MARGARET: Next he'll get an anchor, it'll show he's made of strong stuff. And then maybe another one that says "MOM."

WHEELER: Jesus Christ.

MARGARET: And an eagle's claw on the head of his penis, and when he squeezes it, it flexes its talons.

WHEELER: Margaret, what the hell.

MARGARET: I'm just having fun.

WHEELER: It's not fun. You're acting really cunty.

MINNIE: Wheeler!   MARGARET: Ex*cuse* me?

WHEELER: Give me all the shit you want but don't drag Minnie into it.

MINNIE *(To Wheeler)*: Don't get me into some *thing*—

MARGARET: I didn't say anything about her.

WHEELER: You don't have to, you're just dripping with judgment.

MARGARET: Because I judge you. You've been judged. I feel so freaking sorry for this girl, you have no idea. I don't know how you do it but you've bamboozled another one into buying your shtick, and your shtick is *old* and *tired*.

MINNIE: You're not giving *me* much credit.

MARGARET: No, I'm not.

PAUL: What are you doing?

WHEELER: It's okay, Margaret and I can fight, we've done it before.

PAUL: But it makes me uncomfortable. And when you invited us to a picnic, I said, "Do not go if you're still mad about Jules."

MARGARET: I had every intention of playing nice but just in the last twenty-four hours a couple of things have come up that make that impossible for me.

PAUL: This isn't fair to me. I'm in the middle of this.

MARGARET: You are not. I have my own relationship with Wheeler.

WHEELER: That's right.

MARGARET: I'm not just "Paul's wife" to you, am I, Wheeler?

WHEELER: No, and you never have been.

MARGARET: I talked to Jules and she's having a hard time.

WHEELER: I'm sorry to hear that—

MARGARET: You destroyed her. So it chaps my ass to see you with this girl instead, with whom you have no affinity, no feeling, no empathy, *nothing*.

PAUL: I wish you would stop this now—

WHEELER: You're way off, Margaret. Think I want to be a father just for kicks? She's everything I want in a partner.

MARGARET: She's everything you want in a playmate, someone you can dress up with. You look ridiculous.

WHEELER *(To Minnie)*: My friends think I'm ridiculous.

MARGARET: I talked to Kelly this morning. She tells me you're fighting her in court over child support?

MINNIE: You are?

WHEELER: I'm fighting her *personally* over the definition of alimony. Why are you talking to Kelly?

MARGARET: She wanted some advice about a shrink for Gabe.

WHEELER: Because you know a lot of shrinks for kids. Did it occur to you she called you as a way of getting to me? She's diabolical.

MARGARET: She's scared. Because he refuses to go to school. Were you aware of that? And she checked his computer and found he's watching hardcore porn.

WHEELER: He's a teenager.

MARGARET: Humiliation sites. You know what that means? Sure you do. They're fetish sites for men who get off on seeing women degraded. He belongs to a website, a *pay* site, called "Semen Disposal Units." Women with numbers written on their foreheads. Get the picture? That's your son's childhood.

WHEELER: Oh man, I am not going to stand here in this park on this beautiful day and debate the causes and effects of pornography with you, Margaret.

MARGARET: I could care less about debating that with you. I'm not interested in your ideas. And you certainly know me well enough to know I'm no prude. Anyway, you're a fifty-year-old man, you make your own choices about the things and people you value. But Gabe is fourteen years old.

WHEELER: Now I'm angry. Gabe is none of your business.

MARGARET: Apparently he's none of yours either.

(Silence.)

You wanted to know why I was acting "cunty." Now you know why I can't celebrate the birth of your next child. This champagne tastes dirty to me.

(Margaret exits.
Wheeler and Paul look at each other.
Paul exits.)

SCENE 6

Wheeler's apartment. Later that evening.
  Wheeler is on the phone.

WHEELER: He isn't joining ISIS. He's watching porn. He's not
  the first teenager to look at pornography. *(Listens)* When
  did we lose the ability to make him do what we say? Can't
  you just grab him by the shirt collar and drag him into the
  school? Forget that, I hear how stupid that is.

*(Minnie enters from the bedroom, carrying her laundry basket.
She puts it down, returns to the bedroom.)*

Listen, those bozos work with templates. They collate a
  list of symptoms, then diagnose and label all the students
  who— *(Listens)* You're kidding, "School Refusal Syn-
  drome," what'd I just say?! You can't give it that credence,
  these labels are absurd.

(Minnie returns with hot curlers, a duffel bag. Listens, waits.)

No, I'm not coming over. He won't talk to me, I won't talk to him. *(Listens)* Don't even bring that up with me, that's for the court to sort out. *(Listens)* Yeah, I know, sorry about that but money's tight for me too. And I can't afford to just start floating cash into the ether. Hello? Kelly? Kelly?

(Wheeler hangs up.)

(To Minnie) Are you doing laundry?

MINNIE: I'm leaving.

WHEELER: Where are you going?

MINNIE: Portland.

WHEELER: Oregon.

MINNIE: Is there another one?

WHEELER: Yes.

MINNIE: I'm going to Portland, Oregon.

WHEELER: What's going on?

MINNIE: My friend Dre is moving to Portland. And I'm going with him.

WHEELER: Who the fuck is Dre?

MINNIE: He's a friend from a long time ago. Like a cousin, not like you're thinking. But *Derek's* in Portland. And I need to go see him. I need to see Derek. Not to get back with him but I need to see him and I need him to see me, and see the baby.

WHEELER: He beat you up and left you with nothing.

MINNIE: He's been clean for a couple months now.

WHEELER: How do you know that?

MINNIE: Friends.

WHEELER: Have you been in touch with Derek directly?

MINNIE: Not really.

WHEELER: Not really, what does that mean?

MINNIE: It means not really, we've texted some.

(Pause.)

WHEELER: We've been picking out names.

MINNIE: I know.

WHEELER: Picking out names for our baby.

MINNIE: Wheeler. He's not your baby.

WHEELER: Don't do this.

MINNIE: I'm sorry.

WHEELER: This is a mistake.

MINNIE: Could be.

WHEELER: You told me you loved me.

MINNIE: You made me.

WHEELER: I what? I did? I made you? How did I make you?

MINNIE: Even that first night, it was like, what am I supposed to do? Reject you? Then where am I? I didn't have any place to go, no money, nothing.

WHEELER: So you went to bed with me just for money?

MINNIE: I wasn't thinking of it like that. More like, resistance is futile.

WHEELER: A lot of time has passed since then.

MINNIE: I tried, I was trying! I fooled *myself*. I cooked dinner. I watched those movies and listened to your old music—

WHEELER: Cause we're a couple. That's what couples do. I listened to Vietnamese Psychobilly and you listened to Steely Dan.

MINNIE: It's not who I am. It's not who you are.

WHEELER: Haven't I been good to you?

MINNIE: Yeah.

WHEELER: But you have no reservations about mud-stomping a hole in me.

MINNIE: You wouldn't want me to stay out of some weird obligation.

WHEELER: Aren't people supposed to feel a sense of obligation?

MINNIE: Really, you want me to stay, no matter what the reason.

WHEELER: Yes.

MINNIE: Well, I'm not going to do that.

WHEELER: You don't love me?

MINNIE: I love you as a person.

WHEELER: Really, as a person? Not as a dolphin?

MINNIE: Don't make this hard.

WHEELER: Why shouldn't I make it hard? It should be hard. How long have you been cooking this up? You just woke up today and thought it's time to go.

MINNIE: What Margaret said this afternoon about Gabe, I can't—

WHEELER: I know I haven't been great with Gabe but there's a lot of reasons for that. I'm in love with this baby of ours.

MINNIE: You're in love with some idea about him. But he's gonna be a real person and he's gonna need things. *My* family, we didn't meet each other's expectations, right? Maybe some of that's *my* fault, I mean what they went through, things they sacrificed . . . I have to make good choices for this baby.

WHEELER: Do you have any money?

MINNIE: Not really.

WHEELER: Do you have any plan to make any money? Do you have a *plan*?! What are you going to do when it's time to have this baby?

MINNIE: People figure it out. I have to go.

WHEELER: Please don't go.

MINNIE: I'm sorry.

WHEELER: Minnie, please don't leave me.

MINNIE: I'm sorry.

WHEELER: I'm begging you.

MINNIE: I can't stay here.

WHEELER: I need to tell you something.

MINNIE: Please, Wheeler—

WHEELER: I love you. My God, I'm so in love with you.

MINNIE: No you're not. You're not.

WHEELER: I am, listen to me:

(He gets on his knees, pleads.)

I'm begging you. I'm begging you, just spend the night and let's talk some more, just for the night.

MINNIE: Get up.

WHEELER: Please, I'm begging you.

MINNIE: Please get up.

WHEELER: Just stay the night, one more night, you owe me that, please.

MINNIE: I don't owe you anything.

WHEELER: Please, please, please, please—

MINNIE: I'm leaving.

WHEELER: Let me give you some money.

(Fishes in his pockets, gives her bills. Takes out his wallet, hands her more.)

Hold on, I have more.

(He goes to table, takes all the money from a bank envelope, gives it to her.)

MINNIE: Are you sure?

WHEELER: It's for the baby.

MINNIE: Okay. For the baby.

WHEELER: Can I call you?

MINNIE: Yeah, I guess.

WHEELER: Will you call me?

MINNIE: Do you want me to call you?

WHEELER: I want you to stay.

(Wheeler grabs her wrist.)

MINNIE: Let go of me.

WHEELER: Just stay the night.

MINNIE: Let GO!

WHEELER: I love you.

MINNIE: Let go! Let go of me! *(Breaks free)* Anh không điều khiển em nha! I am a person and I say what I do. Còn anh là ai đây? Anh là ai?

(She leaves . . .)

WHEELER: Listen to me: Minnie. Listen to me:

SCENE 7

Jules sits at her desk in her home office. Wheeler appears.

WHEELER: Surprise. *(Pause)* I wanted to see you. The girl let me in. The young woman.

(He approaches. His limp has grown dramatically worse.)

(With a shrug) The hip is shot, it's fucked, there is no hip. *(Pause)* I just really wanted to see you.

JULES: Why?

WHEELER: I miss you. I feel bad about the way things ended and I wanted to see you again.

JULES: All right. Now what?

WHEELER: I don't know. How have you been?

JULES: Not good.

WHEELER: I'm sorry about that. How's work?

JULES: The same. Busy.

WHEELER: I think maybe I need a life coach.

(Pause.)

JULES: You act like you're waiting for me to talk.

WHEELER: That's not fair. So I have something to say to you then.

JULES: This is the time.

WHEELER: I don't think I . . . *(Pause)* I want to start out right, I can't, there's no way for me to, just in one conversation, explain myself or my particular pathology and I'd sound foolish if I tried, but I did hope . . . I wanted to shed some light, *try* to shed some light on my . . . *(Pause)* Okay, struggling. I feel really bad about the way things ended between us and I wanted to see you and tell you that.

JULES: Which you've now done.

WHEELER: Right.

JULES: Twice.

WHEELER: Yeah, I. *(Pause)* Okay, so, Chicago. This was right after 9/11, which I was profoundly unaffected by, other than confirmation of what I'd been saying for a long time, that Bush and Cheney were a fucking disaster, so I did feel a little smug about that, but still, it's a marker in time, and so right around 9/11, a couple of things happened, and it was kind of a turning point for me, not a good turning point, but at the same time I was going through some turmoil in my career, Kelly and I began this four-year fertility-conception nightmare, and she—

JULES: I'm sorry . . . is this your *monologue*? What's the idea here, that you get to the end of this, and then with this new and more complete understanding of your fucked-up psychology, I'm supposed to, what, *blow* you?

WHEELER: I deserve that, absolutely.

JULES: Deserve *what*? I haven't done anything.

WHEELER: This is not easy.

JULES: Which was harder, dumping me, or this part here?

(Pause.)

WHEELER: We talked about my photography and I was unfair about that, I should've accepted your encouragement.

JULES: Yeah.

WHEELER: You have to understand, after getting shitcanned at the *Sun-Times* and the whole exhibition debacle, I lost faith in myself as a, I don't know, "artist" is too strong, craftsman let's say, "craftsperson." And then Kelly *finally* got pregnant—

JULES: What are you talking about, Wheeler?

WHEELER: I'm trying to explain to you why I made such a stupid mistake when I broke up with you.

JULES: You're doing a terrible job.

WHEELER: If I'm honest with you . . . and there's no reason not to be, but if I'm honest with you, Kelly and I had a good marriage, a little testy maybe, but solid, and then Gabe was born—

JULES: Wheeler, please—

WHEELER: *And then Gabe was born* and I got resentful. Not only of her attention to him, but the structure of our lives, we made this move out here to be close to Kelly's family, and so much of my life seemed to be about just this practical role I had to fill, and I found myself *seething*.

JULES: The point of this is that you have a lot of problems.

WHEELER: Make a long story short, yes, things went off the rails for me, my vocation, my family, my sense of myself, and I was trying not to fall into a trap of doing things just to show my resentment, but I couldn't stop the skid, couldn't seem to get things back in the right—

JULES: You're talking about eighteen years ago.

WHEELER: More or less.

JULES: You've been in a skid for eighteen years.

WHEELER: None of this is coming out the way I hoped. I rehearsed in the car. I even had this fantasy I would sing to you because I remember what you said about how we're supposed to sing, that there's something *freeing* about singing. And *free*, that sounds nice. *(Pause)* But then I thought you'd see through that, that I was using this *tactic* to try to get into your good graces and you might find that off-putting.

JULES: Good instinct.

WHEELER: So I don't know, I thought maybe less is more, and that I should simply say I'm very sorry for the way things ended, for the way I ended things, and that I'd like to see you again, maybe just ease into it, with a lunch, or even just coffee.

JULES: You are mind-boggling.

WHEELER: Thank you.

JULES: It's like you don't even remember me. Like you don't even know who you're talking to. Like you're *alone*. I'm right here. I remember *you*. I remember days and nights we spent together, dates, dinners. Drinks, laughs. Touching. Your smell. Those memories are real. They have meaning for me. But you come here and you pull all this material out of your file cabinet and you might as well be submitting for publication. You really hurt me.

WHEELER: I know.

JULES: I was already hurting. And then you really hurt me again.

WHEELER: I know.

JULES: I assume you and Minnie split up.

WHEELER: Yes.

JULES: What happened, did she not have a good definition of photography? *(Beat)* Y'know, that question, what is photography. I've had a lot of time now to think of a good answer. You know what I think it is? A photograph is a catalyst for seeing beyond yourself. And by that definition, I finally have to agree with you that you're probably not very good at it.

(Pause.)

WHEELER: Minnie left. She left *me*.

JULES: Right.

WHEELER: And I'm pretty blown away by it.

JULES: That stuff is hard.

WHEELER: Yeah. I had started to take on the idea of having a child . . .

JULES: We might have had a child together. Who knows?

WHEELER: We still could.

(Pause.)

JULES: I'm glad you came here, apologized to me. It's meaningful to me. Makes me feel better . . . less crazy. You're probably a decent person. You may not be a psychopath. The jury's out. I don't see the jury coming back anytime soon. I don't see you seeking out the help you need because you're convinced you're always the smartest guy in any room. And maybe you are. You do need to hear me though when I tell you: There is no way on God's green earth I would ever see you again. I could never put myself in that position, knowing what I know about you and the havoc you create. So I accept your apology, and that isn't easy for me because I still feel pretty raw, but it's better for me to just accept it and move on and wish you the best.

WHEELER: That's really unsatisfying.

JULES *(Laughs)*: I'm sure it is.

WHEELER: So even the idea that we might start small, really small, and just have a cup of coffee.

JULES: This is the last time I'm ever seeing you.

WHEELER: Okay. *(Pause)* I could still sing.

JULES: You could but you might embarrass yourself. You should get your hip taken care of.

(Wheeler begins to exit, then stops. Finally, he speaks, quietly, darkly.)

WHEELER: I remember you. I do remember. I remember when you sang that song and sat with me and took my hand and told me I was a turtle who didn't know he'd lost his shell. I was so grateful to you, for seeing me. I felt such relief with you. I fucked it up, something good in my life. I don't know why. But I regret it so much. I do love you. And I believe you love me too.

JULES: It doesn't matter.

WHEELER: Why is that?

JULES: Because I respect myself.

SCENE 8

The camera shop. Wheeler repairs a camera. Anita cleans a display case. Michael sits.
    They work in silence. Finally . . .

MICHAEL: It's quiet in here.
ANITA: I noticed that.
MICHAEL: Normally, you two are a couple of Chatty Cathys.
ANITA: Maybe it's the weather. Feels gloomy out there. Maybe it's just Wednesday.

    (More silence.)

MICHAEL: Anybody watch anything interesting on TV last night?
ANITA: I don't have a TV.
MICHAEL: Why is that?

ANITA: I had one for years but it broke. And I realized how much I didn't miss it.

MICHAEL: You must do a lot of reading.

ANITA: Yeah, I read a lot.

MICHAEL: What are you reading?

ANITA: I'm working through *My Struggle* by that Norwegian guy. I kind of hate it but I kind of love it too. What are you reading?

MICHAEL: I wised up, I only watch TV now.

ANITA: Is that right?

MICHAEL: Every night from seven until midnight. Mother and I.

ANITA: What do you watch?

MICHAEL: Murder mysteries, mainly. Or crime shows, I guess. I'm not sure of the classification. Violent crimes are committed and the perpetrators are pursued and eventually captured. And oftentimes technology is involved.

ANITA: And are these fictional programs or more sort of true crime?

MICHAEL: They seem pretty real. Last night there was a story about a man in Kansas City who kept a sex slave in his basement.

ANITA: Ugh. Those stories give me the creeps.

MICHAEL: He had a relationship with this young woman, he was a friend of her family, maybe. She was young and wholesome and blond-haired and milk-fed. And he had picked this girl up along the road, just giving her a neighborly ride, but instead he took her to his house and locked her in a storage room in his basement, and she lived there with him for many years.

ANITA: Yeah, I hate those stories.

MICHAEL: They had intercourse every day.

ANITA: Right. Well. Wheeler? Watching anything good on TV? Reading any good books?

WHEELER: No.

MICHAEL: He was in love with her. And when they took her away from him, he cried like a baby.

ANITA: Okay.

MICHAEL: Can you imagine that? Being kept in a room and once a day your captor enters to penetrate you?

ANITA: Yeah, no, that's . . .

MICHAEL: I wonder if you'd get to the point where you might start to look forward to him coming in, just as a distraction.

(He points to a spot on the display case in front of him.)

There's a spot right here.

(She cleans the spot in front of him.)

Or maybe she started to care about him. Maybe she started to think about him as a real friend.

ANITA: I don't think so.

MICHAEL: Do you suppose, after all that time, when he would enter the room for her daily penetration, do you suppose she was ever able to have an orgasm?

WHEELER: For the love of Christ, Michael . . .

ANITA: Wheeler—   MICHAEL: What?

WHEELER: Do you even hear yourself?!

MICHAEL: Sorry, have I offended your delicate Victorian sensibilities?

WHEELER: We work with this young woman every day. You don't even seem to register that she's a person, you think she's just some human fuck-toy. My God, are you that afraid of women?

ANITA: It's okay, Wheeler—   MICHAEL: I don't have to justify
                                        myself—

WHEELER: What happened to you? I'm sure your mom did a
    number on you, put clothespins on your little pee-pee or
    something—
MICHAEL: Anita and I are just having a conversation—
WHEELER: You apologize to her right now.

MICHAEL: For *what*?   ANITA: I don't need an
                                        apology—

WHEELER: For being fucking disgusting.
MICHAEL: I only apologize when I've done something wrong.
WHEELER: You worried about your liability? Cause she's got a
    sweet case for harassment if there ever was one—
MICHAEL: Why don't you just get back to work?
WHEELER: Apologize.

MICHAEL: I'm warning you.   ANITA: Wheeler!

WHEELER: *You're* warning *me*, you sick fuck? Apologize to Anita.
ANITA: Please stop this, I don't *want* this—!
MICHAEL: You have worked here a long time and I would hate
    for—
WHEELER: After all the disgusting shit I've had to listen to,
    your sick fantasies about fucking this woman and your
    cum hitting the ceiling and—
MICHAEL: I don't know what you're talking about.
WHEELER: You apologize, Michael.
MICHAEL: Get back to work, or you're fired!
ANITA: Wheeler! Stop!
WHEELER: Apologize!

MICHAEL: This is your last warning!

WHEELER: Fuck you and your warning! Fuck you, Michael!

MICHAEL: That's it, you're fired!

ANITA: No he's not!
No you're not!

WHEELER: Good, fuck you and your fucking lame-ass shop! Fuck you and your mom and your stupid car, I hate your fucking car!

MICHAEL: What about my car?

WHEELER: I don't need this shit job! Nobody uses real cameras anymore anyway!

MICHAEL: What about my car?

WHEELER: If you punish this girl, I'm going to come back and kick your fucking ass!

ANITA: Goddamn it, Wheeler, don't do this!

(Wheeler grabs the Mamiya-Sekor from under the counter.)

MICHAEL: You can't take cameras out of here!

WHEELER: Fuck you I can't, this is my personal camera, you asshole!

MICHAEL: I'm going to need the key to the store.

WHEELER: You need the key, you grimy fuck?! You fucking pig-dog?! I'll give you the key to your *ass*, you fucking prick . . .

(Wheeler struggles to get the key to the store off his key chain.)

ANITA: God*damn* it, Wheeler—!

MICHAEL: I'll send your last check to your apartment.

WHEELER: You better pay me every penny, Michael, you fucking cunt, or I'm coming back here and I'll drag your ass out of this store and throw you into traffic, I swear to God.

MICHAEL: Give me my key and get out of here.

WHEELER: All right, you scumbag prick— *(Still struggling with the key)* —(goddamn this fucking goddamn thing)— *(Finally gets the key off, brandishes it)* —here's your fucking key, but you had better know one thing: I have not received satisfaction!

MICHAEL: What? What does that mean?

(Wheeler cocks his arm.)

No, don't throw it! *(Cowers)* I HAVE NO DEPTH PERCEPTION!

(Wheeler zings the key at him.)

SCENE 9

Lotus Express.
Wheeler sits alone, a tray with a bowl of soup in front of him.
Anita enters.

ANITA: Is *this* what a nervous breakdown looks like? I always
    wondered.

WHEELER: I got your text, you *quit*?! Why did you quit—?

ANITA: I couldn't stay there after you got fired defending me.

WHEELER: But you didn't have to *quit*, you could've figured it
    out—

ANITA: What was I supposed to do, just go back to work like
    nothing happened? You really fucked up.

WHEELER: *I* fucked up, I was helping you, I was trying to
    help—!

ANITA: You think I can't manage Michael? I manage some ver-
    sion of Michael every day. I manage him when I'm in line
    for coffee, when I ride the bus, when I go to the beach.

I managed a lifetime of Michaels before you ever came along.

WHEELER: I was unconscious, I couldn't see anything through the red mist. I wasn't thinking of the repercussions.

ANITA: *Me.* I'm the repercussions. I'm shaky, all right? I . . . I had a relapse. I'm doing my best to keep it together here and . . . I'm trying to keep it together, y'know.

(She breathes.)

"We are not human beings having spiritual experiences; we are spiritual beings having human experiences."

WHEELER: I'm sorry.

ANITA: Yeah, okay.

WHEELER: I am. Really sorry.

ANITA: No, I . . . I know you were trying to . . . whatever. It's okay. Thank you. Oh fuck you, Wheeler. Thank you. Fuck you.

(Pause.)

WHEELER: What're you gonna do now?

ANITA: I need to get my shit together. I've been putting off the decision for a long time but I want to go back to school. I blamed the schools for a long time but the problem hasn't been the schools. It's me.

WHEELER: *How* is it you?

ANITA *(Considers, then)*: Fear. I . . . I have a lot of fear.

(He nods in agreement. He wants to speak. He weeps.)

It's okay. Hey.

WHEELER: Sorry, I've had a rough couple of days.

ANITA: Okay.

WHEELER: I think I need to get my shit together too.

ANITA: Is it your wife? It's not Minnie, is it?

WHEELER: Yeah, she left. It's a lot of things. I've been very foolish.

ANITA: We've all been there.

WHEELER: I got a tattoo. "Minnie." My arm says Minnie.

ANITA: You should put something after it, like "van" or "golf."

WHEELER: Oh fuck. Ow. Ow.

ANITA: "And he was humiliated."

(They laugh.)

"I have not received satisfaction"? What the fuck was that?

WHEELER: It's from *Barry Lyndon*.

ANITA: It scared the shit out of Michael. He thinks it means you're going to do something to his car.

WHEELER: You ever seen that thing? It's a piss yellow '74 Karmann Ghia convertible. Pristine. He's in love with it. He looks so prissy and smug driving that thing, like Elton John on a Shetland pony.

(She laughs.
Nice pause.)

ANITA: It's harder than it looks. Being a person.

WHEELER: Yeah . . .

(Amiable music drifts in from the food court.
Wheeler picks up his camera. Loads it with film, takes off the lens cap, adjusts the light meter . . .)

May I take your picture?

(Anita considers, then . . .)

ANITA: Yep. Yeah.

> *(He points the camera at Anita, focuses . . .*
> *He lowers the camera. Reconsiders.*
> *Reorients the camera for a portrait, leans in . . .*
> *Still not right. Lowers the camera.*
> *Anita is still, unbothered, contemplative.*
> *Wheeler gets out of his chair, kneels, looks through the lens from a lower vantage point . . .*
> *Lowers the camera. Slides the food tray out of his eyeline.*
> *Using the chair to steady his wrist, he brings the camera back to his eye, carefully adjusts the focus . . .*
> *Anita looks directly at Wheeler.*
> *Mona Lisa.*
> *Click.)*

END OF PLAY

TRACY LETTS is a playwright, actor, and resident company member of Steppenwolf Theatre Company. He was awarded the Pulitzer Prize for Drama for *August: Osage County*.